Our Home Is Over Jordan

Our Home Is Over Jordan

A Black Pastoral Theology

HOMER U. ASHBY, JR.

CHALICE
PRESS

ST. LOUIS, MISSOURI

Cover photo: W.P. Wittman Limited
Cover and interior design: Elizabeth Wright

This book is printed on acid-free, recycled paper.

Visit Chalice Press on the World Wide Web at
www.chalicepress.com

10 9 8 7 6 5 4 3 2   05   06   07   08

Library of Congress Cataloging–in–Publication Data

Ashby, Homer U.
   Our home is over Jordan : a Black pastoral theology / Homer U. Ashby, Jr.
      p. cm.
Includes bibliographical references.
   ISBN 0-8272-2718-3 (alk. paper)
   1. Pastoral theology. 2. African Americans–Religion. I. Title.
   BV4011.3.A84 2003
   253'.089'96073–dc21
                                                          2003011294

Printed in the United States of America

To Patsy

�֎ CONTENTS

⊠ ACKNOWLEDGMENTS

While this book is the work of one author, many colleagues and friends have aided in its creation. First, I would like to thank McCormick Theological Seminary for granting me a year's sabbatical to complete the book manuscript. Second, I would like to thank the Society for Pastoral Theology. Each year when this group of pastoral theologians gathers, it has a section on works in progress. At the 2000 annual meeting I had the opportunity to present the initial ideas for this work. Their encouragement and support inspired me to carry on with the project.

As I developed my ideas and thoughts, conversation partners were immensely helpful. Ted Hiebert, Deborah Mullen, and David Daniels, faculty colleagues at McCormick, asked probing questions and recommended resources for me to examine. I am most deeply indebted to Dwight Hopkins at the University of Chicago Divinity School, Chris Schlauch at the Danielson Institute at Boston University, and Ted Campbell, retired Professor of Old Testament at McCormick. Each of them read the first draft of the manuscript and wrote back to me with critical comments and suggestions. I will be forever grateful to them for the time that they took out of their own busy schedules to give me significant feedback in the development of this book.

I would also like to thank my clients, who shall go unnamed but whose life experience as Africans in America gave me crucial insight in both the needs and desires of African Americans for the future. I would also like to give credit to my pastor, Rev. Richard Mosely, and the members of St. James United Methodist Church, whose faith in me has been an inspiration and a confidence-builder. The initial ideas for this book were formed in a class I teach at McCormick on pastoral care in the black church. The students in that course have, over the years, asked critical questions and engaged in significant dialogue about some of the concerns presented here. I am grateful to them for their desire to learn and make a difference in the African American church and community.

My editor, Ulrike Guthrie, has been a blessing from God. Her faith in me and my work, coupled with her excellent editorial skills, have been a major factor in the publication of this book. Finally, I would like to thank my family, especially my wife, Patsy, and my daughter, Jennifer. Their love and support over the years especially during the creation of this work has been appreciated more than I have words to express.

Homer U. Ashby, Jr.

※ INTRODUCTION

During the twentieth century African Americans made steady progress in the struggle for freedom, justice, and equality. The twenty-first century, however, offers no guarantee of similar progress. Currently African Americans are engaged in not only a struggle for freedom, justice, and equality but also a struggle for survival.[1] As Bill Clinton's Initiative on Race report states, "Over the second half of the 20th Century, black Americans have made substantial progress relative to whites in many areas. But this progress generally slowed, or even reversed between the mid-1970s and the early 1990s."[2] In spite of the longest-running economic expansion in United States history, the situation for African Americans, according to many indicators of social and economic well-being, is getting worse.[3]

To refer to the current status of African Americans in America as a struggle to survive may seem alarmist. Yet any number of different observers of the African American situation are beginning to use language that speaks of extremely dire circumstances when it comes to the plight of black America, often using words such as "survival," "epidemic," and "lynching."[4] They report that the injury and assault that African Americans endure in a society dominated by white supremacy has reached epidemic proportions, threatening the health and survival of black people.

Those who would like to put the most positive spin on the advancement of African Americans point to data that suggest that as a group African Americans are faring better than they did twenty-five years ago. However, these figures are misleading. If the data on social and economic well-being

---

[1]Carroll A. Watkins Ali, *Survival and Liberation: Pastoral Theology in African American Context* (St. Louis: Chalice Press, 1999).

[2]Council of Economic Advisers for the President's Initiative on Race, *Changing America: Indicators of Social and Economic Well-Being by Race and Hispanic Origin* (Washington, D.C.: U.S. Government Printing Office, 1998), 2.

[3]Urban League, *State of Black America, 2000* (New York: National Urban League, 2000); and *Changing America*.

[4]Clovis E. Semmes, *Racism, Health and Post-Industrialism: A Theory of African American Health* (Westport, Conn.: Praeger, 1996); Emilie M. Townes, *In a Blaze of Glory: Womanist Spirituality as Social Witness* (Nashville: Abingdon Press, 1995); and Catherine Fisher Collins, ed., *African American Women's Health and Social Issues* (Westport, Conn.: Auburn House, 1996).

for blacks are compared with the data for whites, a different picture emerges. Black progress is really black reversal. A cursory examination of five measures of the status of African Americans at the start of the millennium proves the point. The five measures are: economics, politics, health, cultural identity, and vision for the future.

Economics

As the twenty-first century began, those who were eager to highlight black progress pointed to the fact that black unemployment had dipped below 10 percent for the first time in twenty years. While these figures were accurate, the fact of the matter is that unemployment across the board was at its lowest in twenty years. More to the point, though, is that black unemployment over those twenty years had repeatedly been twice that of whites and that there had been no change in that ratio for the past twenty years. Yes, black unemployment was the lowest it had been in twenty years, but there had been no gain in closing the gap between blacks and whites over that same period.

Twenty percent of young black men are neither in school nor working. This percentage has not fallen over the past ten years. Stagnation is not progress. To remain in the same place over time is to take a step back. Another false indicator of economic gain on the part of black Americans is the poverty rate. The poverty rate for blacks has declined since the early 1990s, a seemingly good and progressive sign. However, from the mid-1970s to the early 1990s the median family income of blacks was stagnant, whereas for whites it generally increased. So again, what appears to be a gain is in fact a loss.

Some economic losses and reversals are so clear-cut there can be no positive spin to cover the reality. Black men's relative pay has declined for at least ten years. This is especially true for college-educated black men, where there has been a 10-percent drop. The same distressing fact regarding pay for black men applies to black women as well. After reaching parity in the mid-1970s, black women's wages have fallen relative to those of white women. A similarly disheartening picture emerges in the realm of politics.

Politics

Across the United States African Americans are underrepresented politically. In 1997, blacks made up 11.8 percent of the 1998 voting age population but numbered only 1.7 percent of all elected officials.[5] At almost every level of government the rate of increase of black elected officials (BEOs) is less now than it was in the 1970s and 1980s. From 1970 to 1990

---

[5]Calculations based on data provided in David A. Bositis, *Black Elected Officials: A Statistical Summary, 1993–97* (Washington, D.C.: Joint Center for Political and Economic Studies Press, 1998).

the average yearly percent increase in federal BEOs was 4.9. From 1991 to 1997 the average percent increase was 1.6, and from 1996 to 1997 there actually was a decrease of 2.4 percent.[6] At the state level the average rate of yearly increase of BEOs was virtually the same from 1970 to 1990 (4.4 percent) as it was from 1991 to 1997 (4.8 percent).[7] The number of BEOs at the municipal level rose each year on average 9.56 percent from 1970 to 1990. From 1991 to 1997 that number had dropped to a yearly average of 1.7.

Further, African Americans are no longer the poster children for civil rights and justice concerns. Where once there was sympathy for the plight of African Americans, there now is resentment about the perceived cost to whites of the black struggle for empowerment. Recent changes in the welfare system, attacks on affirmative action, and judicial decisions on voting rights that discount the tyranny of the majority[8] all have at their core a retreat from a previous era's commitment to full freedom, justice, and equality for blacks.

In addition to the withdrawal of support from the larger society, the withdrawal of blacks from participation in the political system has also contributed to the decline of political influence by blacks in America. Fewer and fewer blacks vote in elections at all levels. It's as if blacks have determined that the political process is not going to work for them. A recent example from my own life illustrates this. The African American electrician I was employing to do some work on my Chicago apartment was telling me about the mentoring role he has tried to play with younger black employees. When he hires a new apprentice, he asks the apprentice to do two things: (1) buy a set of tools (the electrician is willing to help financially with this request), and (2) register to vote. One young man responded to this request, "Aw, I'm not going to register to vote. That won't do anything for me."[9] This attitude is rife in the black community, and there does not seem to be anything afoot to stem the tide of this epidemically rising despair and hopelessness. An even sharper picture of the threat to the survival of African Americans in the twenty-first century is found in the data related to the health of African Americans.

Health

Incredible advances have been made in the sciences of medicine and health care. Yet in spite of these advances African Americans are dying in epidemic proportions from a few particular illnesses and health-related conditions. Infants born to black mothers had the highest rate of infant

---

[6]Ibid.

[7]Ibid.

[8]Lani Guinier, *The Tyranny of the Majority* (New York: Free Press, 1994).

[9]Events in the most recent presidential election only add to this young man's assessment of the futility of voting. Fully one out of every six votes in the African American communities of Chicago were invalidated–that is, not counted.

mortality in 1998, at 13.8 per 1,000 births. This figure is almost double the rate of 7.2 per 1,000 births overall. In no state was the black infant mortality rate below the national average. The black infant mortality rate was highest in Illinois, 17.1 per 1,000 births, and the lowest in Massachusetts, 10.1 per 1,000 births. The leading cause of death for infants born to black mothers was disorders related to low birth weight.[10]

Homicide and HIV/AIDS are the two leading causes of death among blacks aged 15 to 34.[11]   AIDS is the number one cause of death among African American men and women between the ages of 25 and 44,[12] and African Americans under the age of 25 are contracting about two-thirds of the HIV cases in that age group.[13] However, HIV/AIDS is not the only disease that is disproportionately affecting African Americans. While U.S. syphilis rates are the lowest ever recorded, Dr. Helen Gayle, head of the Centers for Disease Control and Prevention's National Center for HIV, STD, and TB Prevention states that syphilis is taking a "staggering toll on the African American community."[14] African Americans have a rate 34 times higher than white Americans. In addition, there appears to be a link between the high rates of infant mortality, HIV, and syphilis. Pregnant women with syphilis have a 40-percent chance of delivering a stillborn child or losing their baby shortly after birth.[15] The Centers for Disease Control and Prevention also point out that having syphilis increases the risk of acquiring and transmitting HIV.[16]

Black men and women have the highest death rates from heart disease and cancer.[17] The rates for all cancers combined were 40 percent higher among black males than white males and 17 percent higher among black females than white females.[18] The highest rate of death due to cancer for blacks resulted from esophageal cancer, with a black/white ratio exceeding threefold in both males and females. Black/white ratios fluctuated between two- and threefold for cancer of the cervix and uterus among females and cancers of the penis, prostate, oral cavity, and stomach among males.[19]

---

[10]The data for infant mortality are from a report titled "Infant Mortality Statistics from the 1998 Period Linked Birth/Infant Death Data Set" by T.J. Mathews, Sally C. Curtin, and Martin F. MacDorman, *NVSR* 48, no. 12, National Center for Health Statistics. The data in the report are based on information from the death certificate linked to the corresponding birth certificate for each infant under one year of age who died in 1998 (www.cdc.gov).

[11]Council of Economic Advisers, *Changing America,* 47.

[12]*Chicago Sun-Times,* 6/02/00.

[13]*Washington Post,* 7/16/00.

[14]Mike Mitka, "U.S. Effort to Eliminate Syphilis Moving Forward," *Journal of the American Medical Association* 283, no. 12 (March 22/29, 2000): 1555.

[15]Ibid.

[16]Ibid.

[17]Council of Economic Advisers, *Changing America,* 48.

[18]National Cancer Institute, Division of Cancer Epidemiology and Genetics, *Atlas of Cancer Mortality in the United States: 1950-1994* (Washington, D.C.: U.S. Government Printing Office, 1999), 36.

[19]Ibid.

And although life expectancy for all races and genders has increased substantially over the past fifty years, the differential gap has remained the same, even widening in the 1980s, particularly for black men.[20]

It is well known that hypertension (high blood pressure) is linked with heart disease, and recent studies have demonstrated that the emotional states of depression and hopelessness (despair) contribute significantly to high blood pressure. A recent study that looked at depression among African Americans estimated that black Americans are two to three times as likely to develop hypertension, and at age twenty-five are twice as likely to have high blood pressure, as their white counterparts.[21] Thus we see that the rise in nihilism among African Americans not only threatens their emotional well-being but also has dire implications for their physical well-being and survival.

Cultural Identity

When it comes to stagnation or reversal in African American achievement related to cultural identity, there are three areas to be noted: (1) the portrayal of blacks in popular American culture, (2) self-esteem among black people, and (3) the absence of a clear articulation of a vision for the future.

In 1953 Ralph Ellison wrote *The Invisible Man,* a book whose premise is that African Americans are invisible in the eyes of the dominant white culture. The unnamed protagonist in the book is portrayed in any number of different circumstances where he is ignored, misunderstood, and otherwise invisible to the whites around him. There is no acknowledgment of him on the street; his voice is not listened to in conversation; and he is disregarded as a customer in stores. His invisibility is the primary feature of his identity. Not only is this individual invisible man invisible, African Americans, collectively, are an invisible people. Daniel Patrick Moynihan's reference to benign neglect as the social policy to employ regarding black social problems is an offshoot of the invisible man perspective.[22] Moynihan considered the social problems facing African Americans to be so intractable that there was little to be done to rectify the situation other than to turn a deaf ear.

The invisibility of black people in American culture has existed from the beginning. African Americans arrived in America before the Mayflower. Much of what is deemed authentically American in American culture grew out of the African American experience, but with little acknowledgment of

---

[20]Council of Economic Advisers,*Changing America,* 44.

[21]Karina Davidson, Bruce S. Jonas, Kim Dixon, and Jerome Markovitz, "Do Depression Symptoms Predict Hypertension Incidence in Young Adults in the CARDIA Study?" *Archives of Internal Medicine* 160 (2000): 1495–1500.

[22]Daniel Patrick Moynihan, "The Negro Family: The Case for National Action," in *The Moynihan Report and the Politics of Controversy,* ed. Lee Rainwater and William L. Yancey (Cambridge, Mass.: MIT Press, 1967).

its black origins. Without the genius and hard work of African Americans, the United States would be far less ahead in its experiment to create a New World and a new society.

During the 1980s and 1990s blacks became even less visible. Numerous television sitcoms featured black stars in the period from 1960 to 1980. Preceded by an era when Nat King Cole was the only black with his own television program and blacks were given only cameo appearances on other shows, the appearance of *Good Times, Julia,* and *The Jeffersons* felt like the floodgates had opened up. Alice Walker, Toni Morrison, and John Wideman were increasingly touted in literary circles. Blacks began to appear more frequently on the movie screen. Although many of the motion pictures portrayed blacks in violent and demeaning images, at least blacks were present in leading roles. And there were a few movies like *Old Yeller* that captured more accurately the full humanity of African Americans. However, by the end of the twentieth century we were once again becoming invisible in the popular culture.

The new season of fall television programs for 1999–2000 offered a clear example of the demise of blacks in the American entertainment scene. As the three major networks began to advertise their new lineups, it became clear that no television program was going to feature a black as its star. Blacks would have minor roles in some of the big hits, but no black would be the featured actor of his or her own show. Organizations such as the NAACP were so outraged by this snub that they encouraged black viewers to boycott the network shows and not purchase the products of their sponsors as a form of protest. Responding to the protest, NBC made an attempt midway through the season to present a show about an inner city hospital, the cast of which had many black actors, but it was pulled before the season ended. Little changed when the new fall season was announced in 2000–2001. Only one show, *Gideon's Crossing,* starring Andre Braugher, had a black as its lead actor.

I should clarify that I am referring to the major networks of ABC, CBS, and NBC. The Fox channel is a whole other reality. In an effort to corner the African American market Fox television has filled its prime time with shows featuring black casts. However, where the majority of Americans go in order to be entertained by television, blacks have virtually disappeared. Two subtle messages are being sent to African Americans: (1) Your insignificance as a participant in the cultural reality of America does not warrant portrayal on the television screen, and (2) your resentment and protest at being ignored is of little concern to us. In both ways African Americans are disregarded and made invisible.

Self-esteem is not an easy variable to measure. Its measurement depends a great deal on one's definition of self-esteem and the instrument that one uses to measure self-esteem. A particular psychometric instrument may be measuring self-esteem based on one set of definitions, whereas another instrument may be measuring self-esteem based on different criteria. There is one measure of self-esteem in the African American community that is certainly quantifiable, although it may not be universally accepted as a reliable indicator, and that is the homicide rate among African Americans, especially African American men. Homicide is the number one cause of death for black males between the ages of 15 and 24. And because most homicide victims are related to their murderer, we can surmise that African Americans commit the vast majority of these murders. African Americans kill one another at alarming rates. The rate of death among African Americans due to homicide is about eight times that of whites.[23]

Black-on-black crime is a form of internalized oppression within the cycle of racial conditioning. As overt and covert forms of oppression are acted out on African Americans by whites, African Americans respond in part by internalizing the oppression they experience. Unable to retaliate effectively, the anger and rage are turned inward. The internalized oppression is both physical and mental. The resulting black-on-black violence bears witness to the internalized oppression. Other factors contribute to the use of violence in interpersonal relationships as well. The stress associated with living in a racist society, along with poor conflict resolution skills, often plays a role in the instigation of violence. Yet alongside all these factors, low self-esteem remains a core precipitating reason in the incidents of black-on-black violence.

Self-esteem is often associated with accomplishment and achievement. When persons take on a challenge and are successful in meeting the demands of that challenge, their confidence in and good feeling about themselves rise. Because the school setting is a primary location for achieving increased self-esteem, the challenges of academic achievement should provide an excellent opportunity to build a sense of competence and self-worth. In fact, one might think that the recent statistics on high school graduation rates for blacks would give some cause for celebration. According to the Bureau of the Census and the National Center for Education Statistics, "The percentage of non-Hispanic blacks aged twenty-five to twenty-nine who have completed high school (87 percent) is nearly as high as that of non-Hispanic whites (93 percent)."[24] The picture begins to dim, though, when we look at the figures for persons aged twenty-five to twenty-nine with a four-year college degree or higher. Although the number of black students completing college increased sharply in the 1960s and early 1970s, those numbers leveled off between the mid-1970s and 1990s. In fact, the number of blacks completing college since 1995 has dropped. And since the mid-1970s the gap between the percentage of whites 25 to 29 who have

---

[23]"Deaths: Final Data for 1997," *National Vital Statistics Reports* 47, no. 19 (June 30, 1999).

[24]Council of Economic Advisers, *Changing America,* 21.

completed college and blacks 25 to 29 who have completed college has increased. What this means is that the increasing number of students who have completed high school are encountering significant failure in college compared with their white counterparts, another sign of stagnation at best and reversal at worst. The implications of such failure certainly impact self-esteem. Since "higher educational attainment is associated with lower unemployment and higher wages, higher family income, and better health for adults and children,"[25] the assault on self-esteem has implications for the whole of the life of the individual.

This pattern of early success followed by subsequent decline in educational attainment begins early for blacks. Black children who attend Head Start programs have a much better chance of doing well as they enter first grade. However, if the additional educational support does not continue, the students begin to flag in their academic achievement and fall behind their larger cohort. To acquire a positive sense of self-esteem throughout the educational system is a constant struggle, a struggle made more difficult by the lack of adequate resources needed to achieve and prosper educationally.

Vision for the Future

What is the vision for the future that will deliver African Americans from the critically dangerous position they are in now? The answer to that question is highly elusive. This dilemma of a clear vision for the future of African American people was not as prevalent thirty years ago. Then most African Americans championed the goals of desegregation, integration, and black power. Today those unifying goals have been replaced with a variety of visions and goals that often conflict with one another and do not have the power to rally a people over a sustained period of time.[26]

In previous decades, a leader in the African American community often provided vision for the future. Not only is leadership in the African American community being redefined, there no longer are larger-than-life

---

[25]Council of Economic Advisers, *Changing America,* 13.

[26]Molefi Asante (*The Afrocentric Idea* [Philadelphia: Temple University Press, 1987], *Afrocentricity* [Trenton: Third World Press, 1988], and *Kemet, Afrocentricity and Knowledge* [Trenton: Third World Press, 1992]) and J. DeOtis Roberts (*Africentric Christianity: A Theological Appraisal for Ministry* [(Valley Forge, Pa.: Judson Press, 2000]) call for an emphasis on the recovery of African roots through Afrocentrism. Victor Anderson (*Beyond Ontological Blackness: An Essay on African American Religious and Cultural Criticism* [New York: Continuum, 1999]) encourages blacks to reject the search for an essential blackness. Dwight N. Hopkins (*Shoes That Fit Our Feet: Sources for a Constructive Black Theology* [Maryknoll, N.Y.: Orbis Press, 1997] and *Down, Up, and Over: Slave Religion and Black Theology* [Minneapolis: Fortress Press, 2000]) suggests that the recovery of the resources of slave religion practiced in the "invisible church" will give new power and direction to the quest for identity and purpose. A number of writers lift up black spirituality, sometimes over against black theology, as the ritual and cultural guide to wholeness and renewal. Implicit in many of these discussions is an underlying debate between the relative merits of cultural renewal versus dismantling oppressive structures.

visionaries like Mary McCleod Bethune, Martin Luther King, Jr., Angela Davis, Stokely Carmichael, and Malcolm X to whom the masses of black people turn for direction and guidance. The one exception is Minister Louis Farrakhan. However, it remains to be seen whether he can capture the imagination of the majority of African Americans and inspire a national movement. Proverbs states that without a vision the people will perish. The lack of a collective vision also threatens the survival of a people who for the past thirty years have been wandering in the wilderness.

Finding Our Way Home

The survival and well-being of African Americans are in jeopardy. On all fronts–economic, political, health, and cultural identity–they are under assault. Such assaults are not new, however. Black people have been engaged in a battle to survive ever since reaching America's shores in Jamestown in 1619. What is different now is that African Americans have drifted into such a state of fragmentation that our survival as a people is at risk. As Ed Wimberly has prophetically and accurately written, African Americans have become "relational refugees."[27] They have become so disconnected from one another that they have lost a sense of peoplehood. Consequently it is much more difficult to withstand the unrelenting assaults a racist society makes on the body and psyche of people of color. Isolated and alone, the individual person is less resourced, is less protected, and more easily singled out for harm and injury. And the threat to survival caused by isolation and disconnectedness is not just external but internal as well. It is a sense of disconnectedness that pushes for individual economic gain at the expense of its impact on brothers and sisters. A fragmented people cannot mobilize politically to exercise their power maximally. They will always be underrepresented. Emotionally distanced from one another, African Americans can more easily kill, infect, ignore, and otherwise disease one another.

A healthy cultural identity is formed in community. Without a collective community there can be no transmission of a healthy sense of self-esteem or self-worth. Especially when a dominant culture is sending messages that constantly undervalue a person's self-worth and identity, there needs to be a counterbalancing force to negate the false images and false definitions that the person is being forced to adopt.

Acknowledgment of and praise for achievements, as well as assistance in accomplishing those achievements, are crucial for healthy, strong self-esteem. Individuals cannot provide these for themselves, especially early in life. Communities of care and nurture provide those necessary ingredients for healthy self-esteem. They pronounce and live out an ethic of care that

---

[27]Edward P. Wimberly, *Relational Refugees: Alienation and Reincorporation in African American Churches and Communities* (Nashville: Abingdon Press, 2000).

guides interpersonal relationships, fosters love, builds compassion, constructs systems of support, and denounces violence and abuse in all their forms. Alone, without any help in charting a course or discerning the terrain, it becomes just about impossible for the individual to find his or her way. Beyond parents and the extended family, mentors and models are needed to provide a full and complete sense of who one is and where one is headed.

Much of what I have described in the above paragraph occurs in homes. Home is where we develop sensitivities and sensibilities about being attached to others. And here I am talking about home in its most positive sense. I realize that many grow up in homes where being a relational refugee is the only way to survive. The home I am envisioning, though, is a home where love, care, nurture, support, and guidance reside. I am also describing a sense of community as home, a home in which persons inspire, encourage, and support one another. The home I have in mind is reflected in the spiritual "Deep River":

> Deep River, my home is over Jordan.
> Deep River, I want to cross over into campground.
> Oh, don't you want to go to that Gospel feast.
> That Promised Land where all is Peace
> Deep River.

The home in "Deep River" is a place of refuge, safety, and protection. It is a place of promise and expectation. Home across the Jordan is where full humanity is realized in the company of others. This kind of home stands as an alternative resistance to the hostile space of a surrounding racist society. It is the home needed by African Americans at this time in the journey. If African Americans do not move soon out of the wilderness where each sheep is going his or her own way, then they, individually and as a people, will perish. Martin echoed the promise of God that we as a people will get to the promised land. It is time, before it is too late, to cross over into Jordan.

The black church has a crucial role to play in the provision of a home where black people in America can have a sense of refuge, safety, and protection; where there is hope and promise instead of despair; where the prospects for survival are enhanced. First, the black church has been engaged in the survival business for a long time. Through the efforts of the "invisible institution" during slavery the African culture of African Americans survived; through its messages of hope and perseverance the spirit of a people survived; through its participation in protests and demonstrations the dignity and power of a people survived. The black church has a proven track record of guaranteeing the survival of black people.

Second, the black church has unique resources for the deliverance of a people from the subtle genocide of these days. It is clear that the enemies of black survival and freedom are not interested in whether black people survive. If black people are going to survive, it will have to be through the prideful efforts they make to secure their own survival in a hostile environment. There may be whites and other allies who help, but in the final analysis it will be important for blacks to take on the campaign for full humanity, because no others will sustain the battle as they will, because their very lives are at stake. Too often African Americans have seen allies turn coat or fall away when their own self-interest is threatened by the survival and liberation of blacks. The spirit of independence, autonomy, and racial commitment is embedded in the history and identity of the black church. The black church owes nothing to the world or earthly powers. It has the freedom to work on behalf of blacks without being beholden to any outside influence.

The black church also participates in what Edward Wimberly calls the "eschatological plot."[28] The biblical narrative is one in which the story of God's people is always in the process of unfolding. No single defeat or downturn marks the end in the eschatological plot. Rather, difficult times or seeming defeats point to a twist in the plot. The divine plan and outcome are still in place, but the way there has been altered. The black church is very much aware of the twists and turns in the eschatological plot. In its preaching, teaching, worship, fellowship, and prayer the black church is constantly reinforcing for its people that black people are God's people and that they live in God's story of ultimate justice and freedom. Survival is guaranteed, and beyond mere survival the battles that they wage for freedom and dignity will result in full humanity.

Third, the black church carries out its ministries in partnership with the living God, whose power has the capacity to will the promises God makes into guaranteed fulfillment. The black church, through its rituals of praise and remembrance, solidifies the relationship with God, who has made promises to black people about the inheritance of full humanity and the guarantee of an abundant life. As the black church maintains that divine/human relationship, then the divinely inspired promise of a new heaven and a new earth will be made real for African Americans.

God has demonstrated in the past this capacity to deliver a people from life-threatening circumstances to a place where they were able to better live out their destiny. We now consider the story of such a deliverance found in the book of Joshua. In Joshua the people of God, who wandered in the wilderness for forty years and nearly perished on the shores of Jordan, are finally led through the Jordan into the promised land. The promised land, their home over Jordan, provides them a place where their well-being is no longer in jeopardy. There, God delivers on past promises, and a people are enabled to claim their inheritance. The promised land offers life beyond mere survival. In this land, flowing with milk and honey, a people come together to experience the health, strength, identity, and future promised by God.

---

[28]Edward P. Wimberly, *African American Pastoral Care* (Nashville: Abingdon Press, 1991), 12–17.

A Response to This Challenge

This book is a response to the threat to survival that confronts African Americans at the present moment. In the following chapters I lift up a biblical image and apply it to what I consider the most significant challenges associated with African American survival: cultural identity confusion, disconnectedness, and the lack of a vision for the future. The biblical image that I am employing is that of the conquest story reported in the book of Joshua. The method that I am using is that of "conjuring"; that is, I am conjuring the story of Joshua to ward off the threat of extinction that is associated with the loss of a cultural identity, the fragmentation of community, and the absence of a vision that gives hope for the future.

The origins of the longstanding tradition of "conjuring" are found in the life and culture of Africans before their transport to America. Conjuring was a means by which Africans brought to bear the power of transcendent forces to affect change in the this-world context. Conjuring produced healing, altered outcomes, precipitated reversals, and otherwise refashioned the course of events. In the history of Africans in America biblical images have frequently been conjured in order to translate and transform African American life. The most frequently used conjure has been the exodus story. The exodus image has shaped a people's identity, has helped explain the nature of their plight, has provided hope for a liberated future, has been a rallying cry for morality and respectability, and has produced what Eddie Glaude has called an "Exodus politics" for nineteenth-century African Americans.[29]

My use of the Joshua story not only reflects the conjuring tradition of African Americans but also participates in the signifying tradition as well. The signifying tradition is that form of African American cultural expression in which an indirect critical judgment is made about a person or circumstance. As a mode of rhetorical interpretation, signifying seeks to reveal or expose meanings and feelings that lie underneath words and actions. At times signifying takes on the form of making fun of a person or situation. At other times it is the capacity to talk around a topic without coming to the point. At still other times it is a game to test the strength of a person to restrain himself or herself in the face of being "screamed" or "sounded" upon. Throughout the course of this book I will be signifying, but not in the sense of it being a game or test. Rather, I will be signifying various other conjured tropes (past and present) in order to make critical judgments about their suitability as interpreters of and visions for the future of African American life in America.[30]

---

[29]Eddie S. Glaude, Jr., *Exodus: Religion, Race, and Nation in Early Nineteenth-Century Black America* (Chicago: The University of Chicago Press, 2000).

[30]In this sense I will be applying signifying in the manner that Henry Louis Gates, Jr., suggests as a metaphor for textual revision, and, I would add, as textual critique. See Henry Louis Gates, Jr., *The Signifying Monkey: A Theory of Afro-American Literary Criticism* (New York: Oxford University Press, 1988), 88.

The Joshua story will play this double role in the chapters that follow. It will be both a conjure and a signifier. In fact, any conjure is necessarily a signifier in that as a conjure is invoked to address a particular condition or circumstance, it critically engages that condition or circumstance in order to expose it to the transformative power of the conjure. My hope is that the Joshua conjure will work optimally as both a transformer of the present reality and critical perspective for the vision of the future.

Other black pastoral theologies have addressed the topics of survival, liberation, disconnectedness, and vision for the future. However, there has not been an attempt to do a critical comparison of these various black pastoral theologies and incorporate them into a comprehensive black pastoral theology. This book undertakes this incorporating enterprise with the aim of identifying those salient themes that are reinforced across the texts. In addition, this is the first time the method of conjuring has been used in a black pastoral theology. And the use of Joshua as a biblical text in black liberation literature in general and black pastoral theologies in particular has never been done before. The hope is that the new ground that this work breaks may be able to free African Americans to think in new and different ways about the current state of affairs and offer new possibilities for future steps, steps that lead to new life rather than annihilation.

Chapter 1 describes the ways in which the Joshua story and its image of the promised land can be a helpful conjurational device for African Americans at this point in their history in America. At a time when the advances in civil rights forged in the mid-twentieth century have foundered in the face of Reaganomics, cries of reverse racism, and attacks on affirmative action, African Americans need a conjure to stem the tide of socioeconomic reversal and growing despair. An examination of the Joshua story's recount of a people who moved out from slavery and annihilation in the desert to claim a home for themselves highlights the key features of this conjure's power to transform and empower, for in the Joshua story a people filled with anxiety and fear are led to a marvelous victory. Not only do they avoid extinction in the desert; they occupy the place of their dreams, a land flowing with milk and honey. There they can not only create a place of their own but also claim the promise of such a home that was promised to them long before. In this sense the ancient Israelites fulfill their destiny. God has promised this home, and the promise comes with an ironclad guarantee. God promises that if the ancient Israelites will have courage and follow God's lead, success and victory are assured. The Joshua conjure holds much promise for African Americans today.

Chapter 2 argues that the survival and liberation struggle outlined in the Joshua conjure has taken on a new form for African Americans at the turn of the twenty-first century. Rather than a single leader like a Joshua, African Americans, as a people, will have to accept the challenge to lead African Americans forward. The lack of an identifiable leader, plus the nature of the campaign itself require that the people as a whole become the chief agents in the struggle. The current challenges require not a Joshua but a Joshua people. The threats to cultural identity, disconnectedness, and lack of vision for the future are best addressed as a people. In the final analysis the collective identity of a people, their connectedness with one another, and their sharing of a common vision will be worked out as a people. Chapter 2 outlines the ways in which the Joshua conjure speaks to these challenges and suggests that the black church can play an important role in supporting a Joshua people in their claim of a home.

Chapters 3, 4, and 5 bring a new approach to the discussion. In each of these chapters I identify what I perceive to be the most critical challenges associated with the themes of cultural identity, connectedness, and vision for the future. After introducing the challenge I then describe the particular way the Joshua conjure addresses the problem and how the black church can be a resource in the process.

Chapter 3 examines the way in which the cultural politics of difference and its related effort to move beyond ontological blackness threaten a cohesive identity for African Americans. The desire to allow for individual differences among African Americans must not occur at the expense of a life-giving collective identity that historically and for the future has the power to inoculate African Americans against the insidious disease of racism. Our self-esteem and worth as individual human beings depend on the health and strength of a cultural tradition that shapes and forms black people into a collective cultural identity.

Chapter 4 examines the many ways in which African Americans are disconnected from one another. The fragmentation occurs on many different levels: age, class, and gender, to name a few. This chapter pays particular attention to the gender divisions that result in African Americans', having the highest divorce rates and the lowest marriage rates in the United States. Again, the conjure of Joshua will be applied to determine whether or not the Joshua story provides insight and direction as to how to overcome this disconnectedness. The black church's role in healing these divisions will also be explored.

Does the claim for reparations represent an adequate vision for the future for African Americans? This is the question addressed in chapter 5. The increasingly loud call for reparations suggests that the future for African Americans rests largely on the payment of the debt for forced labor during slavery. As African Americans move forward into a new promised land, are reparations the best vehicle to move us there? Through examination of the reparations argument in light of the Joshua conjure, I hope to answer these questions and discuss the unique role the black church can play as both place of debate and locus of action.

African American ancestors employed conjures as a way of protecting persons from illness, spells, and the consequences of life. The rituals, incantations, and medicines of conjuring may seem foreign and out of date to the modern African American. However, such conjurational devices in Africa and in America have helped keep a people alive over the centuries. And in light of the failure of more modern socio-political-economic strategies that have been employed, the use of conjuring, and more specifically the conjure of Joshua, may deliver a people from extinction at the shore of Jordan through the Jordan to a place of promise and hope. This book is both a wake-up call and a call to action. African Americans need to begin the campaign before it is too late.

❋ CHAPTER 1

Conjuring the Promised Land

The long-standing tradition of conjuring dates back to the very origins of African peoples. Historian of religion Charles Long describes how in many of the African myths of origin conjuring played a central role in the creation of time, space, and persons.[1] In addition to providing the power to form human beings and their environment, conjures have been viewed and used as medicines to heal illness, allies in the fight to ward off or counter evil spirits, an additional resource to help ensure a desired outcome, and a diviner to predict the future. This list does not exhaust the uses of conjures, but identifies those that are most pertinent to our discussion. The act of conjuring can take many forms, which may be combined in a ritual. Conjuring can take the form of a prayer or petition for a particular god or force to make itself present. Dance or some form of ritual movement can be the medium through which conjuring occurs. Conjuring can include allowing one's self to be taken over by a spirit or force. In most cases conjuring has to do with bringing the conjure in close proximity to a person or situation so as to alter the condition of that person or alter the course of events related to the situation. The need to conjure recognizes that without the input of the conjure, the person or situation lacks what is needed in

---

[1]Charles Long, *Alpha: The Myths of Creation* (Toronto: Collier Books, 1963).

order to bring about the change. The potential power of the conjure released through the practice of conjuring offers the possibility of change.

Not all conjures and not every conjuring ritual produce the hoped-for results. Because some conjures are not as powerful as that which they are being brought up against, the conjuring fails. In other cases an incorrect conjure is used, and a different result emerges than that hoped for. Sometimes the conjure is correct, but the conjuring ritual is flawed. At still other times the particular circumstance requires a careful and nuanced change in either the conjure or the conjuring ritual in order to effectively address a particular situation. If such a change does not take place, the conjure will fail.

Anyone can engage in conjuring. However, in certain complex or difficult situations the expertise of a seasoned conjurer is needed. His or her skill as a delicate master of conjuring can spell the difference between a successful conjure and a failed one. In still other situations a whole people is required to make the conjure effective. At those times the conjure will work best if all are participating in the conjuring process.

In this book I am suggesting that the Joshua conjure, in order for it to be most effective, should be practiced by the whole of the African American community. For ancient Israel, at the time that the book of Joshua was used as a conjure, Joshua was identified as the principal conjuring agent. For African Americans today African American people as a whole will make for the best conjuring agent. The challenges to survival will require no less than the full commitment of a people to thwart annihilation. Individual leaders may be called upon to provide vision and encouragement, but in the end it will be the determination of black people as a people that will win the battle to survive.

My favorite conjuring story in the black cultural tradition is "When People Had Wings." It combines many of the different elements of conjuring highlighted above. In the story a young enslaved African woman with a baby slung over her back begins to physically fade because of the heat and hard work of picking cotton. The white overseer beats her for her lack of production until she is at a point where she cannot go on. She turns to an older slave and asks for relief. The older enslaved African speaks the words "Kuli Ba, Kuli Ba," and immediately the young woman is able to fly above the overseer and the other enslaved Africans. The overseer and his henchman go after the older man, who says the words again. Immediately he and the rest of the enslaved Africans rise and fly off.

At the brink of extinction the young woman is in need of a power beyond herself that will protect her and her child from imminent death. She turns to the conjurer, whose conjuring takes the form of reciting words whose recitation empowers the young woman to fly and escape her impending death. When the conjurer himself is endangered, he speaks the words again; these empower not only him to fly but all the others in the field as well. In the way that the story is told, the conjure is not just the words of the older man. The efficacy of the conjuring is also found in the memories of the slaves. In their remembering what they had forgotten—that they could fly—the power to fly was returned to them. So it was both the words of the older man and the capacity of the people to remember that resulted in their release. In folktales like this and in real life, conjuring has been a means of survival for black folk in America.

As descendants of Africa, African Americans have been able to retain the traditions of African culture, and conjuring in particular has played a crucial role in how African Americans have been able to forge a life and survive in America. African American ancestors employed conjures as a way of protecting persons from illness, spells, and the consequences of life. The conjure of Exodus, for example, gave enslaved Africans meaning and hope. The conjure of Psalm 68:31 by nineteenth-century blacks instilled pride in a people who saw their fight for equality not just as a campaign for themselves, but for the salvation of all humankind.[2] Dr. King's conjure of the image of a beloved community motivated a generation of whites and blacks to establish such a community in America in the twentieth century. The questions that confront us today are: (1) Is conjuring still a viable possibility for twenty-first-century blacks, and (2) what conjuring device has the power to battle the threats to African American survival?

The rituals, incantations, and medicines of conjuring may seem foreign and out of date to the modern African American. However, such conjurational devices in Africa and in America have helped keep a people alive over the centuries. And in light of the failure of more modern socio-political-economic strategies, the use of conjuring, and more specifically the conjure of Joshua, with its emphasis on the success the ancient Israelites had in securing a place of security, ownership, and self-determination, may deliver a people from extinction at the shore of Jordan to a place of promise and hope on the other side. "Conjuring is a magical means of transforming reality," writes Theophus Smith.[3] He argues that African American culture is a conjuring culture in that African Americans have "conjured" various images, stories, and rituals in order to transform the reality in which they lived. Through the power of conjuring, African Americans have been able to magically transform a reality of suffering and oppression into a life and reality of meaning and purpose.[4]

The preeminent conjure text in African American culture has been the exodus story. Slaves conjured exodus in order to affirm two beliefs:

---

[2]Albert J. Raboteau, "*Ethiopia Shall Soon Stretch Forth Her Hands*": *Black Destiny in Nineteenth-Century America* (pamphlet, Tempe, Ariz.: Arizona State University Department of Religious Studies, 1983).

[3]Theophus H. Smith, *Conjuring Culture: Biblical Formations of Black America* (New York: Oxford University Press, 1994), 4.

[4]See Smith's treatment of the extensive way in which the African American conjuring culture has been lived out.

(1) that just as for their counterparts in Egypt, their slavery would not last forever—that there would be freedom some day; and (2) that God was very much aware of their suffering and was on their side. I seek to conjure the promised land as a means for transforming the real threat to African American survival that exists today.

The conjurational image of the promised land that I am drawing on is found in the book of Joshua in the Hebrew Scriptures. There the story is told of the Israelites crossing through the river Jordan to inhabit Canaan, which has been promised to them by God. In the process of acquiring this land "flowing with milk and honey," the Israelites must do battle with the current inhabitants. God promises to assure them victory if they will be strong and courageous and will completely obey God's commands. The first half of the book of Joshua describes the intrigues, battles, and defeats that Joshua and the Israelites encounter in their conquest of the land. The battles are brutal and gruesome. God commands that all the inhabitants of the cities they encounter be killed, including men, women, children, and animals. Nothing is to remain. If anything is left or poached, it is considered *herem* (banned), and its possession is a sign of disobedience. The second half of the book describes the parceling out of the acquired land to the Israelite tribes.

Joshua is called to be the leader of the Canaan conquest. God anoints Joshua to take over the exodus enterprise following the death of Moses. Although Joshua is the leader of the Israelites in the conquest of the land, the composer of the book of Joshua makes clear that God is in charge of the campaign. It is God who is winning the battles, not the Israelites. In fact, God orchestrates the one battle that they initially lose at Ai as punishment for violation by one of the leaders of God's directives regarding *herem*. At the end of the book, Joshua gives a stirring speech to all the people gathered at Shechem. There he recounts with them their history with God and challenges them: "Choose this day whom you will serve, whether the gods your ancestors served in the region beyond the River or the gods of the Amorites in whose land you are living; but as for me and my household, we will serve the LORD" (Josh. 24:15).

From an ethical standpoint a problem arises with the conquest story in its depiction of unprovoked aggression against the inhabitants of Canaan. There is no indication in Joshua that the inhabitants of Canaan were guilty of any provocation against the Israelites such as to warrant the aggression exerted on them. It appears that their only wrongdoing was that they were in the way. How can black people who themselves have been the victims of capricious and arbitrary violence at the hands of a white supremacist society appropriate a story that justifies wholesale slaughter of innocent men, women, and children?

The scholarly evidence suggests that the "invasion" of Canaan may not have occurred as recorded in Joshua. First, some of the cities that were victims of the conquest were not occupied in any significant way at the time accorded to the conquest.[5] In addition, the historical evidence suggests that there had already been an Israelite presence in the region at the time accorded to the "invasion."[6] Israelite presence in Palestine had more to do with the growth of an indigenous Israelite population inside Palestine than a massive immigration of Israelites from outside.[7] Given that there was no invasion or wholesale slaughter of the Canaanites as recorded in the book of Joshua, then Joshua can begin to become a more plausible text to use for conjuring related to the struggles of African American people. But other questions still need to be answered.

Why did the composer of Joshua depict such a gory story for the establishment of a home for the Israelites? Except for Yehezkel Kaufman,[8] who believes Joshua was written close to the time that the events reported in Joshua took place (1200–1175 B.C.E), most Joshua scholars date the writing of Joshua to a much later time.[9] For some it is as early as the time of the exile (550 B.C.E), and for others it is as late as the postexilic period.

The later dating of the Joshua story and the question of whether or not there was an actual conquest are important for our consideration. If the events as depicted in Joshua did not actually take place, Joshua itself can be called a conjure. It is a magical story laced with many miraculous feats whose telling transforms the identity of the ancient Israelites from an enslaved and desperate people to a powerful nation with land and self-determination. The fall of Jericho in Joshua 6:1–27 includes the crumbling of the fortified wall around the city after Joshua and his men march around the walls blowing trumpets made of rams' horns. During a battle with the Amorites Joshua prays to God that the sun not set until full vengeance has been inflicted on Israel's enemies. The exilic/postexilic composers of Joshua conjured the story of conquest in order to transform the reality in which the Israelites were living at the time.

Robert Boling and others surmise that Joshua was composed in the time of King Josiah.[10] At that time the Israelites were a demoralized people who lacked a cohesive identity. The Northern Kingdom of Israel had ended in 721; they were under foreign rule; and they were scattered throughout

---

[5]Richard D. Nelson, *Joshua: A Commentary* (Louisville: Westminster John Knox Press, 1997), 3.

[6]Ibid.

[7]See George E. Mendenhall, "The Hebrew Conquest of Palestine, *The Biblical Archaeologist* 25, no. 3 (September 1962): 66–87.

[8]Yehezkel Kaufman, *The Biblical Account of the Conquest of Canaan* (Jerusalem: The Magnes Press, 1985).

[9]Robert G. Boling, *Joshua* (Garden City, N.Y.: Doubleday, 1982); Adrian H.W. Curtis, *Joshua* (Sheffield, U.K.: Sheffield Academic Press, 1994); Gordon Mitchell, *Together in the Land: A Reading of the Book of Joshua* (Sheffield, England: Sheffield Academic Press, 1993); Nelson, *Joshua*; Lori L. Rowlett, *Joshua and the Rhetoric of Violence: A New Historicist Analysis* (Sheffield, U.K.: Sheffield Academic Press, 1996).

[10]Boling, *Joshua*, and Frank Moore Cross, *Canaanite Myth and Hebrew Epic* (Cambridge, Mass.: Harvard University Press, 1973).

the fertile crescent. When Josiah came to power, it appeared that the fortunes of the Israelites were about to turn. No longer under external domination, Judah was in a position, for the first time in 700 years, to recover a sense of freedom and self-determination. The composer of Joshua was inspired to contribute to the recovery of a sense of peoplehood with the historical/literary product we have come to know as the book of Joshua.

The composer of the first twelve chapters of Joshua is attempting to restore a sense of identity, pride, and power to a people who are on the verge of creating a new reality for themselves. As Nelson writes, Joshua is an "account of Israel's past intended to build and strengthen group identity and explain the contours of its readers present."[11] In short, Joshua is intended to transform the present reality from a time of fear and anxiety to a time of expectation and desire. Joshua is a powerful story of hope in which the promise of God, the will of God, and the guarantees of God all come together to provide a safe haven for a people lost in the wilderness. As the ancient Israelites at the time of Josiah emerge from Assyrian domination, the story of Joshua gives them hope for the future. Joshua reminds them that the promises of God remain true. Although scattered, they have the promise of coming back together to become the great nation that God promised to Abraham. Moreover, God's promise includes God's will to make it happen. However depleted the Israelites may have felt from years of subjugation and oppression, God would more than make up for the lack of resources and capacity to reconstruct the nation. Whatever battles needed to be won, whatever challenges needed to be faced, whatever obstacles stood in the way, the will of God was for the Israelites to reclaim their inheritance. And God would make sure that it occurred. This was the guarantee of God. God's was not an idle promise. The will of God was not going to be held in abeyance. God, acting through the Israelites, delivered on the promise. It was a reciprocal promise and guarantee. If the Israelites would be an obedient, unified, and courageous people in the struggle, God would guarantee through them the restoration of their pride, dignity, and destiny.

Another feature of the Joshua story that makes it particularly helpful for African Americans at this time is that it identifies struggle as a chief factor in any recovery of identity, pride, and empowerment. Deliverance from slavery in Egypt, coupled with the promise of refuge in a land flowing with milk and honey, suggests a time and place of rest and ease. Instead, the Israelites encountered a series of conflicts and battles that were anything but restful. The inheritance of the land required determined struggle. The promise of the land was sure, but the fulfillment of the promise called for active and courageous effort on the part of the Israelites. After they crossed the river Jordan, the image of the promise became realized in the struggle. Although God gave the gift of a place to settle, it was up to the Israelites, in

---

[11]Nelson, *Joshua*, 9.

partnership with God, to make real and concrete the full manifestation of the gift. Without struggle the promise remained unfulfilled. It is not unlike the birth of a child. For nine months the promise of a child grows in the mother's womb. The pain and struggle of "labor" make whole the promise that was in the process of becoming fully realized. Delivery on the promises of God entails struggle on the part of those who seek God's blessing. The struggle does not earn or win fulfillment of the promise. Rather, the promise of God includes dedicated and obedient effort on the part of its beneficiaries in order for the promise to be fulfilled.

Gifts from God should never be taken lightly. The gifts, although freely given, do, in fact, require something of the recipient. First, the gifts require some effort for them to become the gift that they are intended to be. Like those gifts that come with the instructions that "some assembly is required," so, too, with the promises of God. Something in the way of output on our part makes God's promised gift fully given. In the story of Joshua God has promised the land. Yet more is required of the Israelites than crossing through the Jordan. With courage and obedience the Israelites must engage in a series of struggles in order for the gift of land to be realized. God's powerful will guarantees the victories, but without the effort on the part of the Israelites to move beyond mere encampment on the other side of the river, conquest is impossible. Not only would conquest have been impossible, but prolonged encampment at Gilgal would have resulted in death.

Life in the desert wilderness is a struggle to survive. There is little food or water to sustain life. The Israelites had to rely on God's gift of manna from heaven and water extracted from a rock in order to maintain life. The desert wilderness is not a place where one settles, so movement is the norm in the desert, either movement from spot to spot within the desert or movement through the desert on the way to a point beyond. The struggle to establish life outside the desert is a different kind of struggle. It is the struggle to make a place for oneself where none existed before. Sometimes the claiming of place for oneself means resisting hostile forces that would deny one space. At other times it is the struggle to get to the spot where one wants to be, like climbing up a mountain to be on the top. At still other times it means cultivating and nurturing what is already in that place in order to make it useful to one's needs. What one brought along may not fit or be suitable in the new place. The struggle, then, is either to adapt what one has to the environment or decide that because there can be no adaptation, the item has to be discarded. If African Americans continue to wander in the desert wilderness of economic backsliding, political disenfranchisement, serious threats to health, eroding cultural identity, and lack of vision for the future, their fate is doomed. If, however, a new kind of struggle can be mounted, one that moves beyond barely surviving, there can be hope in a new promised land.

So far, for African Americans, deliverance from civil rights discrimination and easier access to the American capitalist economic system have only resulted in escape from Egypt. If the civil rights movement of the 1960s and 1970s constituted escape from Egypt, then the black power and black nationalist movements of the 1980s and early 1990s initiated a plunge into the river Jordan. Pride in one's blackness and recovery of African history and culture emerged as increased black consciousness-raising and Afrocentrism. The black power and other black nationalist movements have moved African Americans closer to the promised land but have not resulted in the full humanity and giftedness that God has promised. Now African Americans remain stagnantly encamped at the edge of the Jordan, not fully cognizant that there has to be movement from this place or they will not survive as a whole people, possessing the full dignity, pride, and destiny God promises. In the face of the threat to their survival, African Americans need a conjure that can spark the transformation from a reality of despair to a reality of hope.

Migration and Wilderness

In her discussion of black migration in African American literature, Farah Jasmine Griffin identifies a four-phase process in the migration narrative: (1) response to a concrete threat, (2) initial encounter with the new environment (usually either the North or the West), (3) negotiation of a response to the new environment, and (4) a choice to either remain or return.[12] The primary threat that sparked Northern and Western migration for blacks was the scourge of lynching. Some have argued that the desire to improve one's economic status was the prime motivator for migration. After all, the great migration of 1910 to 1920 took place during a time when there were abundant jobs in the North because of World War I. Many whites who would ordinarily be at work in Northern factories were fighting in Europe. Because labor was needed in the factories and on the assembly lines, blacks flocked to Northern cities in unprecedented and overwhelming numbers. The opportunities for improving economic status were excellent.

However, Griffin has convincingly argued that the threat of lynching was in fact the chief reason blacks left the South, by showing that there were increased numbers of blacks leaving certain sections of the South where a lynching had recently occurred. In addition, she shows that many of those moments of leaving did not take place during the great migration. She also cites interviews with recent migrants whose stories of why they left point to the violence in the South as the primary reason. The title of Griffin's book is *"Who Set You Flowin?"* She asks, What motivated you to pick up from one place and move to another? What caused you to leave a

---

[12]Farah Jasmine Griffin, *"Who Set You Flowin?": The African-American Migration Narrative* (New York: Oxford University Press, 1995), 3.

place that was familiar to enter into a place unknown to you? Why would you embark on a journey filled with potential danger, pain, and hardship? What caused you to take such risks? The questioner assumes that there must be a very important motivator for making such a monumental move. Traveling to an unknown place, leaving friends and family, and altering the course of one's life require a very significant reason. In the case of the black migrant that reason was life itself. In order to preserve life in the face of brutal and arbitrary violence, blacks flowed to the North, where they presumed that there would be greater safety and protection. The prevalence of lynching was not nearly as extensive in the North. And so when a friend or relative was lynched, the wish to preserve one's life prompted the black migrant to set out on the journey away from death.

In a variety of ways blacks are being lynched at the beginning of the twenty-first century. There is the lynching of economic strangulation, the lynching of political disenfranchisement, the lynching of higher morbidity, the lynching of the loss of cultural identity, and the lynching of perishing because of lack of vision. Emilie M. Townes describes in detail the lynching of African Americans through actions and policies that threaten the physical health of the black community.[13] She is particularly concerned about the placement of toxic waste management facilities close to poor, black neighborhoods. These communities are particularly vulnerable to this kind of lynching because impoverished black communities often do not have the economic base to adequately support their public services. Schools, roads, water treatment, and other infrastructure systems go wanting because of a lack of municipal resources and capital. When a waste treatment company proposes to build a plant in or near those communities, with the prospect of increasing the tax base, the offer is almost irresistible. With promises that the company will provide jobs and be environmentally safe, residents choose to ensure the "survival" of their communities by embracing what appears to be a safe action. Not until later do these communities come to find that the cost to their health far outweighs the benefits of additional tax dollars and jobs. Lynching these days is a much more subtle and complex venture than it was a century ago. Instead of a rope, policies and systems are used to strangle the life out of African American communities. Black bodies no longer swing from trees like some strange fruit. Instead, black bodies are deprived of essential, life-sustaining nutrients (physical, emotional, political) or infected with death-causing diseases and public policy decisions.

Because the lynchings that occur now are not as visible as they have been in the past, there has not been the same kind of mass response to move away from harm. Blacks remain camped at Gilgal, languishing in

---

[13]Emilie M. Townes, *In a Blaze of Glory: Womanist Spirituality as Social Witness* (Nashville: Abingdon Press, 1995).

hopelessness and despair, seemingly unable to protect themselves from a ravaging racist environment or to move to a more life-giving place. *What will set blacks flowing?*

Part of the motivation for writing this book is to increase the consciousness of African Americans and their allies that the wholesale well-being and survival of African Americans are in jeopardy. Things are not as good as some project. The data that I presented in the Introduction suggest that an immediate, large-scale effort needs to be mounted to counter the downward spiral that is emerging in the life of the African American community. Now is the time to act. If the downward spiral gains greater momentum, there may not be the resources or the human will to stem the tide. If the current reversal trends continue, blacks may become so focused on survival that there may not be enough residual energy to give toward living beyond survival. And if the white majority deem that the "problem" is too big to solve, then reverting again to some form of distancing (red-lining, suburban flight, gated communities, and "benign neglect") may occur. The outcome for African Americans will be mere survival at best and extinction at worst. A friend of mine, a gastroenterologist who sees many black patients with diseases of the intestinal system caused by the disproportionate rates of high blood pressure, diabetes, and cancer in the black community, has commented, "After a while, the only black person you will be able to see will be stuffed and on display in a museum."

In the Joshua story the Israelites found fulfillment of the promise in the occupation of the land. A people who had wandered in the wilderness for forty years were finally going to have a place to settle, to call home. There they would no longer be as vulnerable to the dangers and threats of the wilderness. The promised land offered a more safe and dependable environment.

But there was more than that. In the wilderness a whole generation had grown up disconnected from the cultural rituals that gave them an identity as a people. So one of the first acts of occupying the land as a people was the renewal of the circumcision ritual. When Joshua reinstituted the circumcision ritual as a part of the conquest venture, he conjured the idea that conquest of the land was not limited to physical warfare and battle. A people's claim on the inheritance of a land promised to them included reclaiming a sense of who they were. The space to be claimed was not just a parcel of land but an identity as a people found in the interiority of their souls and psyches—their consciousness. So we see throughout the book of Joshua that Joshua leads the people through periodic rituals and recitations regarding their identity. Before crossing the Jordan, Joshua entreats the people to sanctify themselves (Josh. 3:5). In this ritual of purification the ancient Israelites prepare for the wonders that God will do among them. As they enter into the Jordan, the ark of the covenant precedes them. The Ark is held in the midst of the Jordan while the people pass in front of it, reminding them of their covenant with God and linking that covenant with their entrance into Canaan.

After crossing, Joshua directs the leaders of the twelve tribes to erect a memorial made of stones to remember this event in the people's history. This is done so that when their children ask, "What do these stones mean?" another opportunity arises for the people to recall their history and thereby solidify their identity. The battle narratives are interspersed with rituals of remembrance and commitment. The keeping of the Passover, the ritual march around the walls of Jericho, the disbursement of the land, and the renewal of the covenant at the end of Joshua are all examples of ritual conjuring in order to empower the ancient Israelites in their campaign.

In the midst of a life-threatening time and place, African Americans must likewise find a place that will be life-sustaining and that will protect them from the kinds of lynchings that are threatening their existence. That place is not so much a physical place, for there is no place in America where racism does not exist—it is systemic. There is no nirvana where blacks can escape the ravages of racism. Instead, the promised land for blacks today needs to be found in an internal consciousness. This internal consciousness is characterized by an increased sensitivity to the threat of extinction, the restoration of a sense of collective identity, engagement in an ongoing struggle beyond mere survival, and partnership with God in whom the will and the guarantee of the promise are located.

The promised land that the Israelites occupied was not new territory to them. Canaan had been home to the earlier descendants of Abraham (Deut. 8:1). Entering the promised land, then, was a return home. The promise of a home for the Israelites operated at two levels. On one level Joshua and the people were to occupy a land flowing with milk and honey. At another level the promise of a home for the ancient Israelites was linked to a previous promise that the descendants of Abraham would be more numerous than the stars in the sky. The promised land became the place where such nation-building could be established.

In this new century the promised land that African Americans must enter is not a new place. Rather, the promised land is a place that African Americans have occupied before. The history and identity of African Americans did not begin with slavery in America. Their long and rich cultural tradition begins in Africa and reflects a people with dignity, self-determination, and full humanity. At various times in the journey toward freedom and justice African Americans have sensed a threat to their full humanity and have mobilized massive resistance responses. At times those responses have been armed conflict in the form of slave revolts. At other times the response has been to flee violence and murder through migration. And at still other times the response has been to remain on the American scene but fashion a unique way of being African American in America through creative expression of what it means to be black in America.

Orlando Patterson states that African Americans at the present moment are the most disconnected group in American society and the most disconnected in the history of their presence in America.[14] Particularly along gender lines and class lines African Americans exist with large chasms carved throughout their community. They are increasingly choosing not to marry and are more inclined to seek divorce than they were fifty years ago. William Julius Wilson and the National Urban League have also documented the growing split between African Americans with means and those in the underclass.[15] Obviously there have been times in African Americans' past where there was greater connectedness and shared life together. Much of the shared life in close proximity to one another was the result of segregation and discrimination. Yet whatever the various contributing factors, African Americans found ways to cooperatively and creatively build institutions, establish effective mediating structures to buffer the effects of racism, and foster a sense of hope and meaning. A recovery of this sense of connectedness is desperately needed.

In the struggle for full humanity that has been an ongoing enterprise for blacks since setting foot on American soil such a sense of connectedness has waxed and waned. Through the glorious victories and ignominious defeats the battle for full humanity continues to be waged, fueled by the formidable presence of hope. That hope has been recited in any number of folk sayings over the years: "Trouble don't last always," "Trouble in mind and I'm blue, but I won't be blue always. Sun gonna shine in my back door someday." This hope and belief in better times yet to come have sustained a people through some of the most inhuman assaults upon body and psyche. But what happens when that hope begins to disappear, when nihilism and despair occupy the space where hope once resided? The answer is that the struggle wanes. The effort to love one another diminishes. The capacity to stay connected to one another decreases. A people who struggled mightily to advance together become increasingly preoccupied with individual advancement and achievement. To stem the tide of recent reversals in health and well-being, a return to the disciplines of struggle that have brought African Americans thus far by faith is desperately required.

The perspectives of the Christian faith have provided invaluable resources for the freedom struggle for African Americans. Whether it was conjurational stories from the Bible or inspirational music adapted to become freedom songs, belief in God who sided with them has been a chief resource for African Americans in their quest to survive and find full humanity in America.

---

[14]Orlando Patterson, *Rituals of Blood: Consequences of Slavery in Two American Centuries* (Washington, D.C.: Civitas/Counterpoint, 1998).

[15]Lee A. Daniels, ed., *The State of Black America 2000: Blacks in the New Millennium* (New York: National Urban League, 2000); and William Julius Wilson, *The Truly Disadvantaged: The Inner City, The Underclass, and Public Policy* (Chicago: University of Chicago Press, 1987).

Yet the presence of such a belief is not as prevalent now. Jeremiah Wright, pastor of Trinity United Church of Christ in Chicago, told me about a conversation he had with some teens in his church during a regular forum he holds with them called "Pizza with the Pastor." He reports that the teenagers had a difficult time describing how God played a role in helping them to deal with the pressures in their life. When it came to peer pressure associated with drugs, gang intimidation, performing well in school, and dealing with sexual urges, God was not a ready resource in their minds. When it came to the interpersonal conflicts in their homes, many of the teenagers were not wondering how God was present but wondered if God was present at all.

In the pastoral counseling that I do, this lack of reliance on God is not restricted to adolescents. Many adults are oblivious to the presence of God in their daily lives. A return to the promised land for African Americans also means a return to witnessing to the fact that God is most truly present in the ongoing struggle for freedom, dignity, and full humanity.

Promised Land or Land of Broken Promises?

Not everyone has such a hopeful perspective, however, and some are downright critical about the promised land image. To conjure the promised land image is also to signify—that is, to engage in critical judgment about other images or objections to the promise land image. One such act of signifying comes from Charles Shelby Rooks, who presents the strongest critique of using the promised land image for the African American freedom struggle.[16] Rooks argues that America has not been a promised land for blacks. Writing in 1973, Rooks, like many others, was beginning to sense the collapse of the hopefulness that radiated in the 1960s victories of the civil rights movement. The 1972 election of Richard Nixon, coupled with the cries of reverse discrimination, heralded a less enthusiastic and more hostile attitude nationally toward black social and economic achievement. From a historical perspective the African American experience in America was composed of a number of unfulfilled promises. Blacks discovered that the Voting Rights Act of 1964 had a shelf life of twenty-five years, urban renewal was becoming black removal, and there were calls for the reexamination of affirmative action initiatives. King's dream of an American society where blacks and whites shared equal justice, opportunity, and rights was rapidly becoming a nightmare.

Rooks suggests that the image of diaspora is more fitting for the African American experience. Stolen from their homelands in Africa, African Americans reside in America as part of the larger African diaspora. As a people in diaspora, African Americans are separated from their homelands

---

[16]Charles Shelby Rooks, "Toward the Promised Land: An Analysis of the Religious Experience of Black America," *The Black Church* 2, 1 (September 1973) *Chicago Theological Seminary Register.*

and their cultures, alienated from other Africans in diaspora, despised by a dominant culture that is hostile to their presence, and fighting to preserve a sense of identity. For Rooks the diaspora image not only describes the black situation in America but also reflects an attitude of despair and hopelessness. In diaspora, African Americans have not only been taken from their homes and cultures but are no longer able to put their hope in the new place to which they have been brought. Diaspora in America is a lonely and mournful existence. African Americans will strive and barely survive but will never thrive in diaspora. In a prophetic way Rooks in 1973 began to speak to the pervasive hopelessness that Cornel West and others identified some twenty years later.

Prior to Rooks there were other critics of the promised land image, whose critique grew out of a desire to counter the prevalent negative images of blacks. In their writing and preaching, nineteenth-century African American scholars sought to build up pride and dignity in African Americans by making a deliberate connection between African Americans and the people of Egypt, Cush, Ethiopia, and Canaan. The identification they made was not with the Israelites but with the kingdoms and peoples of Northern Africa and the eastern coast of the Mediterranean Sea. Albert J. Raboteau writes of them:

> Nineteenth-century black Americans identified Ethiopia and Egypt with their own African origins and looked to those ancient civilizations as exemplars of a glorious African past, surely as fictive a pedigree as American claims of descent from Graeco-Roman civilization…From the Egyptians the torch of civilization passed on to the Greeks, from them to the Romans, and from the Romans, finally, and belatedly, to the Europeans.[17]

Gayraud Wilmore indicates that the identification with the Canaanites not only sought to challenge negative stereotypes of blacks but also countered an identification with the Israelites. Their work confronted

> the testimony of many books and pamphlets arguing for black inferiority, stubbornly relied upon what has been an ineradicable feature of black religion in America: an interpretation of scripture rooted and grounded in the corporate experiences and perceptions of blacks. They identified themselves with the Canaanites, who built great cities across the Jordan and resisted the invading Israelites for centuries; with the Carthaginians, who produced Hamlicar and Hannibal and were related to the descendants of the Canaanites; with Nimrod, the great Cushite hunter and warrior whose might founded cities and conquered others from Babel to

---

[17]Raboteau, *"Ethiopia Shall Soon Stretch Forth Her Hands,"* 5.

Nineveh; but most of all they identified themselves with Egypt and Ethiopia–the two great African monarchies that were the incubators of much of what is called Western culture and civilization.[18]

Given Rooks's negative evaluation of the promised land image and the indirect critique of identification with the Israelites found in nineteenth-century African American literature, can and should African Americans adopt the promised land image as a helpful conjurational image for the turn of the century? I still think so. For Rooks is writing about America as the promised land, but America is not the promised land I am proposing. In fact, the promised land I am proposing stands over against the false promises and threats to survival that are embedded in American society for blacks. The promised land for blacks in the twenty-first century is a place that exists within the larger American society and its culture but at the same time maintains a separate existence. This separate existence is more attitudinal than spatial. The promised land is an attitude, a way of being, a responsive resistance, but yet an a priori declaration of what it means to be black in America. Such a promised land is rooted in the promise, will, and guarantee of God. The promise is that African Americans as a people can live a life with full humanity, that God will supply the power and the will for black people to struggle in this conquest, and that the victory of full humanity is guaranteed even in the face of a hostile, death-dealing environment.

African Americans, along with many others of African descent, are indeed in diaspora. I am not sure, though, that diaspora should be the defining image for African Americans. The sorrowful and disempowering image of a people scattered and separated from what gives them their identity is a disheartening one. Rooks's depiction of the diaspora existence is accurate. Such an image evokes feelings of despair and hopelessness. The depressing strains in Psalm 137 give witness to that despair. In addition, the diaspora image provides little in the way of a plan of action in response to the despair and hopelessness. It is as if diaspora is a permanent condition from which there is no remedy or escape. In the Bible the only hopeful outcome is a return to Jerusalem, but the return of African Americans to Africa as their salvation is not a viable option in the twenty-first century. African Americans are no longer Africans in the same sense that today's inhabitants of Africa are Africans. Numerous stories, a mixture of humor and pathos, are told of zealous and dedicated African Americans returning to live in Africa and failing miserably to make the transition.[19] Although

---

[18]Gayraud S. Wilmore, *Black Religion and Black Radicalism,* 2d ed. (Maryknoll, N.Y.: Orbis Books, 1983), 121.

[19]Randall Kenan, *Walking on Water: Black American Lives at the Turn of the Twenty-first Century* (New York: Vintage Books, 2000).

some African Americans have successfully transplanted themselves—and W. E. B. DuBois is a prime example—his story is one of a few over against a number of stories of disappointment and disillusionment on the part of both Africans and African Americans.

Nineteenth-century African American scholars and preachers were focused on the task of countering negative stereotypes of African Americans by the dominant society. More specifically, they were attempting to counter the Hamitic curse that was used as a defense for slavery and as support for the view that blacks were inferior human beings. Today there is not the same need to defend against the perceived inferiority of black people. Although there still exist radical white supremacists and a few scientists who subscribe to the inferiority of blacks, that viewpoint is not as dominant as it has been in the past.[20] Blacks need not feel caught in a bind of needing to reject identification with the ancient Israelites in Joshua in order to retain a positive sense of black identity as descendants of Africa and Canaan.

The exodus story has played a central role in the survival of blacks in America. First, the exodus story provided a narrative mirror of the lives of the slaves. "It required no stretch of the imagination to see the trials of the Israelites as paralleling the trials of the slaves, Pharaoh and his army as oppressors, and Egyptland as the South."[21] Through the story of the plight of the Israelites African Americans could see their own experience and thereby gain an interpretive perspective on that experience. Such an interpretive perspective laid the foundation for deriving meaning and understanding of that experience.

Second, the liberating version of the exodus story appropriated by enslaved Africans provided an antidote to the toxic interpretations of the Bible that were used to enslave the minds, souls, and bodies of blacks. Robert Franklin identifies this counterinterpretive use of the exodus story in much of black preaching:

> For instance, preachers have employed the exodus motif, the most famous in black sermonic discourse, to portray the African American struggle for justice as continuous with, and parallel to, ancient Israel's struggle to escape from Egypt. Portraying the black experience through this biblical lens offered a bold and prophetic challenge to the primary assumption of American civil religion, namely that America was the new Israel sent on an "errand into the wilderness" to establish a free, God-fearing nation. Black preachers transgressed the dominant narrative, characterizing

---

[20]Effective responses to Arthur Jensen's "Bell Curve Theory" can be found in Russell Jacoby and Naomi Glauberman, *The Bell Curve Debate: History, Documents, Opinions* (New York: Times Books, 1995), and Steven Fraser, ed., *The Bell Curve Wars: Race, Intelligence, and the Future of America* (New York: Basic Books, 1995).

[21]Langston Hughes and Arna Bontemps, eds., *The Book of Negro Folklore* (New York: Dodd, Mead, 1958), 286.

America as the new Egypt guilty of oppressing a new generation of slaves.[22]

The exodus story has also been a vehicle for the expression of black protest without unduly risking the lives of African Americans. Timothy Smith writes, "The Christian beliefs [the slaves] adopted enabled the African exiles to endure slavery precisely because these beliefs supported their moral revulsion toward it and promised eventual deliverance from it without demanding that they risk their lives in immediate resistance."[23] Referring specifically to the exodus narrative, James Evans observes:

> The exodus motif furnished an acceptable expressive vehicle for the slaves' yearning for political emancipation. While the sustaining resources of traditional African religion had been driven underground by the system of slavery, the Bible, read in this way, provided the means for asserting that freedom was a central thrust in the biblical narrative.[24]

The exodus story has provided meaningful insight, countered spurious interpretations of the biblical text, and enabled the safe expression of resistance. With such a rich legacy of contribution to the African American struggle for freedom and liberation, why abandon the exodus motif for the promised land image?

The exodus motif functions more as a signification of what African Americans are fleeing from rather than an indicator of what African Americans are moving toward. The exodus story is limited in its focus because it brings African Americans out from bondage, but does not bring them into a full possession of that freedom. In Egypt, African Americans were slaves; now that African Americans are free, who are they? For the past century African Americans have been working at shaking off the vestiges of their slave existence. The ravages of slavery will never be completed healed or eliminated, so in that sense African Americans will always be engaged in a process of freeing themselves from the debilitating remnants of the past. However, it is time now for African Americans to find ways of living in America defined not by who they were but who they are to become.

Just as slavery in Egypt and wandering in the wilderness were deviations from God's original plan for the descendants of Abraham and Sarah, so, too, were slavery in America and the wanderings of the past fifty years

---

[22]Robert M. Franklin, *Another Day's Journey: Black Churches Confronting the American Crisis* (Minneapolis: Fortress Press, 1997), 40–41.

[23]Timothy L. Smith, "Slavery and Theology: The Emergence of Black Christian Consciousness in 19th Century America," *Church History* 41 (1972): 498.

[24]James H. Evans, Jr., *We Have Been Believers: An African-American Systematic Theology* (Minneapolis: Fortress Press, 1992), 41.

deviations from God's plan for African Americans. It is God's desire that African Americans live in the fullness of their humanity with dignity, pride, and freedom. Their destiny is not to live so far behind whites in terms of life achievements and at the bottom of almost every index of socioeconomic status. Joshua stands as a conjure for the transformation of a people from slavery to freedom, from wilderness wandering to the establishment of a home. Joshua also stands as a signifier against the threat to survival of God's people of African descent. As conjure and signifier Joshua leads African Americans to a new phase of peoplehood characterized by a strong cultural identity, a committed connectedness to one another, and a hopeful vision for the future.

CHAPTER 2

The Joshua Church

In their monumental study of the black church in the African American experience, C. Eric Lincoln and Lawrence Mamiya employ a dialectical model in their social analysis of the black church: "Black churches are institutions that are involved in a constant series of dialectical tensions. The dialectic holds polar opposites in tension, constantly shifting between the polarities in historical time."[1] They identify six main pairs of dialectically related polar opposites:

1. The dialectic between priestly and prophetic functions.
2. The dialectic between otherworldly and this-worldly.
3. The dialectic between universalism and particularism.
4. The dialectic between the communal and the privatistic.
5. The dialectic between charismatic and bureaucratic.
6. The dialectic between resistance and accommodation.

Although each of these dialectic tensions bears import for the issues raised thus far in this book, I want to focus here on the first.

---

[1] C. Eric Lincoln and Lawrence H. Mamiya, *The Black Church in the African American Experience* (Durham, N.C.: Duke University Press, 1990), 11.

Lincoln and Mamiya define the priestly function of the black church as a maintenance function, a function that addresses the worship and spiritual needs of its members. The prophetic function, on the other hand, leads to involvement in more political concerns and participation in the affairs of the larger community. Later and throughout the remainder of the book Lincoln and Mamiya identify the priestly functions as focused on survival and the prophetic functions as focused on liberation. The black church is always engaged in both survival and liberation; at any given moment in its history, though, the black church may be more concerned with survival or liberation. To the extent that African Americans are engaged in a struggle for survival as outlined in the Introduction and encouraged in chapter 1 to adopt the Joshua image as a resource for both survival and liberation, it would be helpful to examine the nature of the survival and liberation functions of the black church.

Whereas Lincoln and Mamiya present the priestly and prophetic functions as a dialectic, Gayraud Wilmore views survival and liberation as overlapping and intertwined. Wilmore writes:

> What may be called the liberation tradition in black religion also begins with the determination to survive, but because it is exterior rather than primarily interior (and for that reason its carriers find more space in which to maneuver) it goes beyond strategies of sheer survival to strategies of elevation—from "make do" to "must do more." Both strategies are basic to Afro-American life and culture. They are intertwined in complex ways throughout the history of the diaspora. Both are responses to reality in a dominating white world. Both arise from the same religious sensibility and inheritance that took institutional form in Afro-Christian and Afro-Islamic cults and sects from the mid-eighteenth century onward.[2]

From Wilmore's perspective mere survival is a political act. Survival becomes a political act as it challenges dehumanizing treatment that threatens to deny physical existence to blacks. In this sense to survive is to resist. Survival also acts as a political strategy in that it produces future generations who will engage in the struggle for freedom and justice. The political victory may not come in the present moment, but by surviving, real hope remains alive for victory in the future.

Carroll A. Watkins Ali does not reference Lincoln and Mamiya but adopts the same words of survival and liberation as cornerstones for her pastoral theology in African American context.[3] Like Lincoln and Mamiya,

---

[2]Gayraud Wilmore, *Black Religion and Black Radicalism: An Interpretation of the Religious History of Afro-American People*, 2d ed. (Maryknoll, N.Y.: Orbis Books, 1983), 227.

[3]Carroll A. Watkins Ali, *Survival and Liberation: Pastoral Theology in African American Context* (St. Louis: Chalice Press, 1999). In formulating her thoughts about what is meant by survival and liberation, Ali has drawn upon bell hooks, *Sisters of the Yam* (Boston: South End Press, 1993), and Vincent Harding, *Hope and History* (Maryknoll, N.Y.: Orbis Books, 1990).

Watkins Ali views survival and liberation as critical elements in the African American experience. "Descendants of African people, who arrived on the shores of North America as import for slave trade, have sustained a struggle for *survival and liberation* in this sector of the world for nearly four hundred years."[4] Watkins Ali provides the following definitions of what she means by survival and liberation:

> What is meant by the term *survival* is the ability of African Americans (1) to resist systematic oppression and genocide and (2) to recover the self, which entails a psychological recovery from the abuse and dehumanization of political oppression and exploitation as well as recovery of African heritage, culture, and values that were repressed during slavery. By liberation, I mean (1) total freedom from all kinds of oppression for African descendants of slaves and (2) the ability of African Americans as a people to self-determine and engage in the process of transformation of the dominant oppressive culture through political resistance.[5]

Even more than Wilmore, Watkins Ali views survival and liberation as incorporating elements of one another. For Watkins Ali survival is resistance to political oppression that entails recovery *from* psychological abuse and dehumanization, as well as recovery *of* African heritage, culture, and values. Conversely, liberation is a survival strategy in which African Americans live free, free from oppression with self-determination. Liberation is a state of enhanced survival. From these definitions of survival and liberation, Watkins Ali suggests a comprehensive and expanded pastoral theology that emanates from the indigenous experience of African Americans, emphasizes the communal versus the individualistic approach to pastoral care, and expands the functions of ministry in such a way that they are nurturing, empowering, and liberating in praxis.

In the Introduction two of the survival concerns listed deal with the concrete and practical issues of health and economics. The other three survival concerns (politics, cultural identity, and vision for the future) represent construction of the self (collectively and individually), interests that Wilmore and Watkins Ali identify in their discussions of survival and liberation. This construction of the self, which is part of a survival strategy, has two dimensions.

The first dimension is the recovery of an identity that is one's own. For four hundred years Africans in America who have become African Americans have been victims of negative characterization. Slaves were not considered human beings. They were property to be bought and sold. There was debate as to whether or not slaves had human feelings and

---

[4]Ali, *Survival and Liberation*, 1.
[5]Ibid., 2.

sensibilities. When it came to calculating their humanity in the United States Constitution, blacks were originally counted as only three-fifths human. Until fifty years ago African Americans did not name themselves. Niggers and Negroes were the names given to black people. Often depicted in literature and American popular culture as mentally deficient, cowardly, superstitious, and lazy, blacks have been engaged in a constant struggle to counter these racial stereotypes since having been brought to America. It has been a struggle to remember and recover a sense of self that reflects the autonomy and pride blacks had as a people in Africa.

The second dimension of the survival strategy is the actualization of the recovered self. This is manifested in political and cultural empowerment that is able to ward off attacks on the positive sense of self-identity generated by the dominant culture. Throughout the course of African American history blacks have encountered various attempts at political and cultural disempowerment. At times blacks are made to be an invisible people whose very existence is denied. At still other times their presence on the political and cultural landscape is recognized but is short-lived, and often compromised. During Reconstruction blacks occupied significant numbers of legislative offices in the U.S. Congress and state houses. This spate of black political power was brief because of Southern vigilantes and the eroding influence of Northern carpetbaggers. A century later in the 1970s and 1980s a number of urban centers elected black mayors. Their ascendancy to power was linked to white flight from cities, which resulted in depleted tax bases. Although the political clout was present to elect a black mayor, the mayors found themselves overseeing cities whose lack of financial resources threatened the economic viability of those very same cities.

I have already highlighted the alternating cultural pattern of blacks portrayed in popular culture as either stereotypically vulgar and morally deficient or absent from the stage at all. A more recent depiction of blacks in popular culture is that of magical helpers who exist solely to redeem or save the white hero or heroine.[6] In these depictions the black helpers are never fully developed as human personalities. They have no family, no history, no roots, and no interests apart from their role as helper. They survive only to the extent that they serve the advancement and well-being of their white helpees. An actualized, recovered self for African Americans would mean a people whose identity is determined and named by themselves, whose purpose and destiny as a people is shaped by their discernment with one another and their God. This is the life that Jesus talks about in John 10:10. It is not just *a* life, but *the* life. Such a life is more than mere survival. It is a life that is *abundant.*

---

[6]As in movies such as *The Legend of Bagger Vance* or *Shawshank Redemption.*

Survival that takes the form of a recovered authentic self and an actualization of one's own identity and purpose is primarily an interior process. A people who have truly survived have been able to maintain their history and heritage within them. Recovery for them is an ongoing process in which there are regular times and practiced rituals for recovery of the collective self. Whenever and wherever persons gather, they recount the stories that constitute their heritage, culture, and values. As individuals, families, and groups they affirm on a regular basis who they are and where they are headed. With clarity about self and purpose, they are then ready to live out in concrete action their identity and their destiny.

These concrete actions flow from the interior processes of self-formation and make themselves manifest in exterior campaigns of liberation. Understood in this way, survival is a necessary precursor to liberation. Without a clear sense of identity and destiny it is impossible to act with the necessary internal fortitude to engage in resistance and transformation. A prerequisite to liberation is time and energy devoted to the survival functions. The liberation functions rest upon the survival functions in order to bring them to full and satisfactory completion.

Here is where I differ from Lincoln and Mamiya on the relationship between the priestly or survival functions and the prophetic or liberation functions. They are not polar opposites in tension (conflict) with each other, but complementary dimensions of a dynamic cycle whose energy requires a rhythmic flow between the two. The survival function possesses nascent elements of liberation that evolve into concrete political actions that make visible and whole the identity and destiny of a people. Likewise, the liberation actions, institutions, and initiatives of a people must continually return to the interior processes associated with survival in order to set proper direction and remain vital. It is my contention that African Americans at the beginning of the twenty-first century have been engaged for the past fifty years in a liberation enterprise without paying sufficient attention to the survival function. Consequently, both the survival and liberation of African Americans have suffered.

Survival Strategies at the Beginning of the Twenty-first Century

In their social analysis of the black church, Lincoln and Mamiya identify two crucial challenges facing the black church in the near future: (1) church life and programs that address the African American poor and underclass; and (2) ministry to young adults and youth.

> The gradual emergence of two fairly distinct black Americas along class lines—of two nations within a nation—has raised a serious challenge to the Black Church...The challenge for the future is whether black clergy and their churches will attempt to transcend class boundaries and reach out to the poor, as these class lines

continue to solidify with demographic changes in black communities.[7]

Citing the work of William Julius Wilson and other social scientists, Lincoln and Mamiya conclude that the black churches' historical role in uplift and advocacy for those most at risk in American society should move the black church to attend to this most vulnerable group of African Americans. Recognizing that many historically black churches are not attracting younger blacks, Lincoln and Mamiya suggest that the black church redouble its efforts to reach out to youth and young adults. These two areas of concern overlap in that many black youth grow up in poverty and that the financial success of many young, well-educated blacks has contributed to a growing gap between affluent and less well-off blacks. The real danger that I see facing the black community and therefore the black church is the bifurcation of African Americans into separate groups, or nations, as Lincoln and Mamiya indicate.

The survival and liberation of black people have always depended on their solidarity. As slaves, blacks gathered together in the "invisible church" of the brush in order to comfort, sustain, and encourage one another. There blacks collectively called on God to attend to their plight and apply a balm in Gilead. During the great migration African Americans provided shelter, food, clothing, money, and their spiritual homes to one another in order to ease the burden of the transition from South to North. During the civil rights movement blacks banded together to march, ride, sit, and protest against discrimination. Without these collective efforts blacks would not have survived. The prospect, then, of African Americans dividing up into separate groups, losing a sense of connectedness and responsibility to one another, is troubling and fearsome.

Many African Americans are troubled by this. In addition to church historians, pastoral theologians have identified alienation and disconnectedness as important areas of concern for black churches and their ministries. Edward Wimberly suggests that an increasing number of persons in the society in general and the African American community in particular have become what he calls "relational refugees."

> Relational refugees are persons not grounded in nurturing or liberating relationships. They are detached and without significant connections with others who promote self-development. They lack a warm relational environment in which to define and nurture their self-identity. As a consequence, they withdraw into destructive relationships that exacerbate rather than alleviate their predicament.[8]

---

[7]Lincoln and Mamiya, *The Black Church in the African American Experience,* 384.

[8]Edward Wimberly, *Relational Refugees: Alienation and Reincorporation in African American Churches and Communities* (Nashville: Abingdon Press, 2000), 20.

The relational refugee is marked by two mutually reinforcing traits: (1) alienation from others, and (2) a sense of self-sufficiency. The relational refugee chooses to live a solitary existence. Because relationships in the past have been disappointing or painful, avoiding relationships is a means by which one sidesteps such disappointment and pain. Without meaningful, helpful relationships the relational refugee is often in a position of having to go it alone. The thinking is that because I as a relational refugee can achieve many things by myself, I do not need anyone else. This belief system then comes around full circle and returns to the belief that I do not need to be in relationship with others. This reinforcing cycle of alienation and self-sufficiency creates persons who are vulnerable to depression, despair, grandiosity, and loneliness. Wimberly argues that such persons are in need of nurturing relationships that can heal old relationship wounds, provide new models of how to relate, and create safe and reliable environments for reaching out to and relying on others.

A mentoring relationship is the nurturing relationship that Wimberly offers as the healing aid for relational refugees. Such a mentoring relationship is not new in the African American experience. The extended family tradition within the African American community has fostered the development of many mentoring relationships that have been crucial in the survival of blacks in America. However, modern American culture's emphasis on individualism and individual achievement has lured African Americans into adopting values that threaten the affirmation of extended family and mentoring relationships. African Americans need to recover the mentoring tradition that has been a mainstay for the survival of a people over the past four hundred years.

Lee Butler has also identified interpersonal relationships as a crucial area of pastoral concern in the African American context. He highlights the relationship between black men and black women as an important focus for the black church and its clergy. Butler argues that the treatment of blacks in America has had a devastating impact on their ability to form the kind of loving, caring, supportive family relationships African Americans would like to have.

> If we look at the historical foundations of our relationships, it is not difficult to see why we treat one another the ways we do. When we look at our relationships through the lenses of the dungeons and Middle Passage, it is no surprise that African American women and men are searching for home. Women have made reclaiming sacred selfhood a high priority due to the violations of their bodies. Men continue to struggle with issues of control and respect because of their inability to function as patriarchs in a patriarchal world. This also makes it easier for us to understand why we have the sex and gender identities we do. The degree to which our gender identities have been constructed around the experience of our

brutalization affects all of our relationships-brother/sister, covenantal, familial, communal, and societal.[9]

Again, in accord with the resistance and recovery survival model proposed by Watkins Ali, Butler argues that African American men and women in their marriages and families must resist the dominant culture's estimation of blacks–their culture, beliefs, family patterns, and ways of responding to protracted traumatic experiences. To resist the dominant culture's past treatment and current evaluations is to recover the sense of community found in African spirituality. Butler refers to this recovery process as a search for home. The search for home as a journey and a process includes a number of elements:

- Becoming equal partners in relationships: concerned, committed, and supportive of one another
- Unifying our spirituality and sexuality so that we do not make the split that the spiritual life is good and the sexual life is bad
- Ending the separation of black church from community so that both together can participate in the salvation of the black community
- Nurturing the extended family so that it is a resource for health and wholeness
- Transforming African American manhood and womanhood so that African American men and women relate to one another with a respect for differences and an appreciation of one another's gifts[10]

Whereas Butler relies on the image of "home" to talk about the processes of survival and liberation for African American families, Archie Smith, Jr., employs the image of "the river"[11]:

I use the river metaphor in several ways. First, I use it as a metaphor for the workings of American society as a whole…Second, I use the river as a description of family life process, and for the ongoing life of individual family members…Third, I refer to all families as rivers that have their differing points of origin within the wider, multicultural society in general and black culture in particular.[12]

American society is the large river system within which the stream of African American family life flows. The African American family acts as a critical guiding current within the larger river system to aid persons in

---

[9]Lee H. Butler, Jr., *A Loving Home: Caring for African American Marriage and Families* (Cleveland: Pilgrim Press, 2000), 36.

[10]Ibid.

[11]Archie Smith, Jr., *Navigating the Deep River: Spirituality in African American Families* (Cleveland: United Church Press, 1997).

[12]Ibid., xxxi.

avoiding disaster. That disaster can take many forms. The American mainstream flows in waters that include dangerous obstacles of racism, classism, and sexism. African Americans have suffered mightily flowing in this American mainstream. As blacks attempted to flow more easily and successfully in this mainstream through integration and assimilation, there were terrible consequences for African American cultural pride and self-esteem. Blacks employed skin-whitening creams to make themselves look more white. Survival and advancement depended on being docile, passive, and subservient. If a black was perceived as assertive, the label of "uppity Negro" was applied, and any chance for favor from the larger society was denied. And perhaps most pernicious of all was the message in the mainstream that the failure to thrive as a people was due to laziness and lack of effort on the part of African Americans. No attention to the faults and discrepancies within the system itself were allowed. Consequently, African Americans constantly find themselves battling against a history of "an internalized sense of black inferiority, a belief in white superiority, and the idea that black people with their culture and history have contributed nothing to advance humankind."[13]

That is why Smith proposes that any pastoral care in the African American church and community have two foci: strengthening African American families as they combat the culturally debilitating effects of the American mainstream and encouraging them to resist and transform the larger system itself. The African American family has a crucial role to play in preparing individuals to do battle with the forces within the larger mainstream that have the potential to destroy positive self-identity and render individuals powerless to alter the current. Without the power to fight those destructive mainstream forces, African Americans are like a piece of driftwood, carried wherever the river wants to take them against their own will, dashed upon the rocks of racism, classism, and sexism until they are battered, bruised, and splintered.

The African American family and the larger African American community have the responsibility to equip persons for the challenges they must face every day in the American mainstream. The African American family should be that place where a strong sense of black pride is built so as to counter the disparaging assessments of what it means to be black, as well as to encourage black persons to challenge any systemic effort to denigrate or diminish the identity or culture of black people. Smith offers three key resources for African American families and communities to adopt in their navigation preparation: (1) dimension of depth, (2) reflexivity, and (3) sense of agency.

---

[13]Ibid., 16.

The dimension of depth is the African American family's capacity to draw on the spiritual legacy found in African American history, culture, and freedom struggles. The dimension of depth represents those spiritual forces that surround and flow within African American families to extend their temporal power as they confront earthly challenges that have a spiritual dimension. African Americans are engaged in spiritual warfare when dealing with the forces of racism, classism, and sexism. These evils will not be successfully fought with earthly power but must be engaged with spiritual power–a spiritual power that has sustained a people's survival in the face of overwhelming odds and circumstances.

Reflexivity is the capacity to respond creatively and imaginatively to the external circumstances that surround a people or persons. Reflexivity involves dreaming, envisioning, conjuring, thinking critically, and making do. Reflexivity in a family is its way of finding a way to respond to any given situation so as to maintain the family's survival and sense of well-being to the greatest extent possible.

To have a sense of agency is to believe that one can act in such a way as to bring about a change or a difference. For me a sense of agency is an important ingredient for hope. Hopelessness is often associated with the inability to believe in or effect change. The situation that one is in may feel interminable and not likely to change. Hope emerges out of a sense that things can change and, more importantly, that there is something that one can do to bring about the change. Full or complete hope rests on both the potential for change *and* the ability to bring it about. Limited hope is that hope in which there is the potential for change but no ability to bring it about. Under those circumstances hope depends on luck, or someone else's doing, but the dependence on someone or something else limits the confidence one can put in that hope. Hope, however, that includes both the potential for change and the capacity to bring it about is a hope in which one can put full confidence. In that kind of hope all the ingredients are in place for change to occur. Moreover, with a sense of agency one can not only effect change, but, because of the power to influence the outcome, can more confidently determine the outcome. African American families with a sense of agency can direct the flow of the river and affect the influence the larger American society river system has on the flow of the stream of the African American family.

Smith further claims that there is a spiritual dimension to each of these resources for navigation. The dimension of depth carries the spiritual legacy of African American history, culture, and freedom struggles. The words of the spiritual song "He's Never Failed Us Yet" reflect this spiritual dimension of their legacy as a people:.

> Leaning on the Lord,
> trusting in his holy power,
> he's never failed us yet.

Oh, Oh, Oh, Oh, Oh, Oh, Oh,
he'll come around,
he's never failed us yet.

Historically, African Americans have always turned to God as a source of power in difficult times. God has always come through. The African American family must continue to tell the stories of God's ever-present power and encourage family members to trust in and lean on God. The spiritual dimension of reflexivity is found in the African American saying, "God may not be there when we want him, but he's always on time." This God works in partnership with African Americans to work toward deliverance and liberation. The flexibility inherent in reflexivity requires that African Americans be able to transcend their own limited and fixed ways of responding to a situation. That transcendent realm is where the answers to survival and liberation reside. If African Americans can direct their vision to the solution that God has in mind, or wait patiently until God's perfect timing, the *kairos* moment arrives, then a more favorable outcome will occur. The spiritual dimension of a sense of agency is found in the African American saying, "God will make a way out of no-way." In this saying African Americans identify a resource for full and complete hope. Where there appears to be no possibility for change, God is a resource guaranteeing that change will come. The spiritual resources associated with dimension of depth, reflexivity, and sense of agency constitute the spiritual legacy and force necessary for navigating the treacherous waters of the American mainstream.

Smith bemoans the fact that many African Americans are cut off from the spiritual resources they need for successfully navigating the deep river. He identifies these persons as "spiritual refugees" whose status can result from a number of factors. Some African American families do not actively lift up the African American spiritual legacy in their families. Driven by secular concerns for materialistic acquisition and individual achievement, these families do not promote African American history, culture, and values. Children and young adults in these families grow up without hearing the stories and participating in the rituals that linked them solidly to the spiritual resources of their heritage. In some cases the black church has not fully welcomed all African Americans to their houses of worship so that they could avail themselves of the spiritual resources to be found there.

Smith is particularly troubled by the black churches' lack of openness to gay and lesbian parishioners. Lincoln and Mamiya similarly point to the black churches' need to do better out reach to urban youth and the poor. Gays, lesbians, urban youth, and the poor who feel alienated from the black church are more likely to become spiritual refugees. Smith further challenges the black church to work intentionally with African American families to strengthen their spiritual resources of dimension of depth, reflexivity, and a sense of agency, as well as to make these resources available to all members of the larger African American family.

Returning to the Story of Joshua

Chapter 1 included an introduction to the Joshua story and offered that conquest narrative as a conjurational resource for African Americans at the beginning of the twenty-first century. In that introduction I summarized the story of Joshua and discussed its usefulness for the current struggles facing African Americans. I want to reintroduce the Joshua story at this point to determine how it might assist in some of the survival strategies that have been explored previously. In this treatment of the story I want to focus on the level of the story that lies below the level of mere narrative of events. The story is one of conquest. But as we have seen, it is also a story of identity, promise, fulfillment, and guarantee. Moreover, it is a story whose conjurational power can transform a given situation so that survival resists annihilation and liberation overcomes enslavement. At this deeper level the Joshua story offers concrete action strategies and conceptual frameworks for the survival and liberation of African American people.

Any time we as individuals or a group embark on a new enterprise there are always fear and anxiety, which are associated with a number of different possibilities and questions: What will we encounter? Will it be too much for us? Will we be successful? Do we have the resources necessary to succeed? Will we be hurt? How long will it take? Will we run out of energy? The initial impetus to undertake the project is full of hope, anticipation, and delight. Indeed, this was the case for the ancient Israelites. For forty years these people had suffered the physical and emotional hardship of the wilderness, but God's steadfast protection and promise enabled them to overcome these hardships. They awaited the fulfillment of the promise, and it kept them going. But just as they began the enterprise, the feelings of fear and anxiety came to the forefront.

God must have sensed that this state of fear and anxiety was beginning to grip the ancient Israelites as they were encamped on the western side of the Jordan River in Transjordan. Consequently, God gave a message to Joshua to address the Israelites' fear and anxiety. The message was in the form of an ironclad guarantee that they would be successful in the acquisition of the promise that God made to them. Before they have even taken the first step across the Jordan, God tells them that the land is theirs already: "Cross the Jordan, you and all this people, into the land that I am giving to them...Every place that the sole of your foot will tread upon I have given to you" (Josh. 1:2–3). This is no hollow promise. It is a promise that comes with a guarantee. This is a "done deal." In this promise the past, the present, and the future are fused. It is not a matter of what God *will* do, but a matter of what God *has already done*. The conquest has been achieved, and so the promise is already fulfilled; the promise, then, is a sure one.

African Americans live in an age now where such promises and guarantees are not assured. In a society dominated by investment capital strategies for getting ahead, the promises are often hedged with qualifiers:

"Past performance is not a guarantee of future yields." As a people African Americans have seen the promise of racial equality and justice reneged on. Like Langston Hughes's raisin in the sun, the dreams of black people for full humanity have not been fulfilled. The promises of God are of a vastly different ilk. God's promise is a past promise that will be fulfilled in the present/future. Moreover, it is a complete and comprehensive promise: "No one shall be able to stand against you all the days of your life. As I was with Moses, so I will be with you; I will not fail you or forsake you" (Josh. 1:5). The inheritance that has been promised carries with it a guarantee that applies for all time and under all circumstances. God ends with this pronouncement about hope: "Be strong and couragous; do not be frightened or dismayed; for the LORD your God is with you wherever you go" (1:9). In a time when many of the indices of social and economic well-being for African Americans show either stagnation or reversal, resulting in a growing nihilism, blacks need the promise and hope found in this first chapter of Joshua. God's promises will not fail. They carry the assurance and guarantee that eliminate fear and despair. In God's promises the future outcome has already been fulfilled. There is no need to worry or be anxious, because God's all-encompassing promise is realized even in the present moment.

Is this a message that the black church can with integrity give to single black mothers gripped by poverty, or young brothers addicted to cocaine, or black urban professionals climbing the corporate ladder? Might it sound hollow and false in the face of adversity or irrelevant in the face of market realities? I think not. There is a deep need for a promise that can truly be fulfilled. Whether that promise is for a better life, freedom from addiction, or more meaning in life, African Americans need a promise giver who is trustworthy. Fear, anxiety, and hopelessness are, in part, the result of hopes and dreams that have been shattered because of false promises. Belief in the fulfillment of promises is foundational to the will to survive and the struggle for liberation. Without the sense of a promised future in which there will be a difference, there is little motivation to survive. Suicidal thinking assumes that the pain and misery of the present moment will not abate but will only stay the same or get worse. Rather than survive with unrelenting suffering and pain, suicide is chosen as a response to the absence of the hope and promise of a better future. One can see why nihilism within the black community has emerged to the extent that it has. The decrease in socioeconomic well-being in the black community points to a future where matters will not get better.

Black churches have a crucial role to play in the restoration of hope. As stewards of the divine promise, black churches carry within their very being the essence of hope. Black churches do this in a couple of ways: First, the black church is the community's memory of the mighty acts God has performed in the past to ensure (guarantee) the survival and liberation of black folk. In fact, the black church has been a primary agent in the deliverance of blacks over the centuries. Not only has the black church recounted the stories of God's deliverance, it has been the very vehicle through which those stories have been acted out. The witness of the black church is that God delivers on promises. God has done so in the past for African Americans and will continue to do so in the future. At this point God is speaking to African Americans not through a Joshua, but through a Joshua church.

This shift is consistent with the narrative in Joshua in which God's marching orders are transferred from Joshua to the ancient Israelites as a whole. Although God initially calls Joshua, God's intent is for the call to go forth to the whole of the nation. Today the black church is the conveyer of the message—the conjurer who proclaims that God's promises are sure, yesterday, today, and tomorrow. The black church has historically made this proclamation but needs to make it even more forcefully now in the wake of a series of socioeconomic reversals at the end of the twentieth century and the potential for even further reversals in light of a new government in Washington at the beginning of the twenty-first century. In this present time of fear and anxiety about the future, the black church is God's servant to rally a people to not be dismayed but to "be strong and courageous" (Josh. 1:9).

Second, the black church leads in the way of true hope, and there are a variety of ways in which hope can manifest itself. True hope in the African American Christian context relies on God as the promise keeper. Other ways of hope represent only false hope in that they do not rely on God or God's promises. In most cases these false hopes rely on promises that carry with them neither the power of will nor the guarantee of success that God does. In Joshua the inheritance of the promised land does not depend on the force or the might of the Israelites. Rather, the inheritance of the promised land is rooted in the primacy, power, and guarantee of God. The Israelites need only align themselves with the will of God and victory is theirs. As African Americans continue in the struggle for survival and liberation in the twenty-first century, it will be imperative for the black church to share its ongoing message of God's guaranteed promises.

Encamped on the Shores of the Jordan

At the beginning of a new millennium African Americans find themselves encamped on the shores of the Jordan. Freed from slavery in the nineteenth century, African Americans since then have been engaged in a freedom journey toward full humanity. The elimination of Jim Crow laws, the acquisition of the right to vote, the abolishment of the separate-but-equal arrangement, and other civil rights attainments have moved them further along. However, they are not there yet.

Most recently the promised land of full humanity has seemed less of a possibility. The journey has not been forward, but backward. Camped at the shore of the Jordan African Americans seem to be a people divided, lost and without hope. To complete what was begun at the time of emancipation and to bring to fulfillment what God has in store for African Americans, there needs to be a crossing over into Canaan and a claiming of the inheritance. In the story of Joshua that enterprise was composed of gruesome battles against the present inhabitants of the land. For African Americans today the conquest enterprise is different. The battles are no less intense, but they take a different form. The challenge today is to secure an identity as a people, become more connected as a people, and develop a vision for the future for this people.

Identity

When Watkins Ali refers to the need for African Americans to recover a sense of self and to recover their African history, culture, and values, she is referring to important psychological features of identity formation. A person's identity, who that person understands himself or herself to be, is composed of a sense of self shaped by the history, culture, and values of his or her culture group.

One of the ways that the identity issue has emerged recently for African Americans is found in the question, "What does it mean to be black at the start of a new century?" The search for identity has many dimensions. One dimension has to do with how one names oneself. Up until the latter part of the twentieth century others named blacks in America. African Americans have been niggers, colored, and Negroes. In the 1970s blacks began to name themselves. Since then they have been black, Afro-American, and African American. At its heart this naming of themselves is a search for identity. It is a search for who and what they know themselves to be. Named by others, black identity is determined by others. Named by themselves, they determine their own identity.

What they call themselves, in many ways, determines who they are. Their identity, though, is more than what they call themselves. Black identity also has to do with what one identifies with. In some cases the litmus test for being black has had to do with identification with a particular goal or agenda, such as integration versus black power. In other cases the determination of one's blackness has had to do with alliance with a particular black leader–say Al Sharpton versus Jesse Jackson. In some cases the determination of blackness has had to do with physical appearance: skin color, facial features, hair texture. Sometimes the determination of blackness has been based upon how one carries oneself: the King's English versus Ebonics, how one walks, the deference one gives to whites. All these features and more have been used in the black community to assess a member's blackness. The issue of blackness is important because it not only determines who African Americans are but, more important, who they are to become, where they are headed.

It is this forward-looking dimension of identity that is linked to the third dimension of living into a vision for the future. Where a people will ultimately wind up is a crucial element in the formation of identity. Who blacks hope to become shapes the current activities, rituals, behavior, preparation, and disciplines necessary for the achievement of those goals. And clearly identity has much to do with one's connectedness to others. None of us creates our own identity. Our identity is very much influenced by the persons with whom and the culture and environment in which we grow and develop. Oftentimes the search for identity as it relates to issues of connectedness is fraught with tension and conflict. The individual person struggles with how much the influence from those around him or her will determine his or her identity. All these dynamics are a part of the search for identity and are currently active in the African American community in particular ways. Chapter 3 will explore one of these issues: the desire to move beyond ontological blackness. But before delving into that topic, it is necessary to examine what Joshua may have to contribute to twenty-first-century African Americans' search for identity.

Joshua and Identity

In Joshua the primary identity feature of the people of God is that they live in the destiny that God has for them. Their destiny is to live as a free people who have control and self-determination in the place where they reside. This destiny has a past, a present, and a future. Thus the conquest of the promised land is actually a return to the promised land. Where Moses and Joshua are leading the people is where God had promised a home to Abraham and Abraham's descendants. Abraham had previously resided in the land that the Joshua generation is going to occupy. Thus the destiny of the people of God in Joshua is a destiny that has been fixed in the past. It is also a destiny rooted in the here and now, because there are battles to be won in the present moment in order for the destiny to be fulfilled. In particular, the battles in Canaan are a means through which the destiny of ancient Israel is to be accomplished.

The story in Joshua is also a story of future destiny. As ancient Israel struggles in the present to claim the land that had been promised in the past, it establishes a place in the future for its freedom and self-determination. The true fulfillment of the promise lies in the ongoing survival and liberation of the people of God in the place that God has promised to them.

What is the destiny that God desires and promises to African Americans yesterday, today, and tomorrow? It is full humanity. I agree with Dwight Hopkins and other black theologians who identify this as the goal that God has in mind for African Americans.[14] Full humanity includes all the

---

[14]Dwight N. Hopkins, *Introducing Black Theology of Liberation* (Maryknoll, N.Y.: Orbis Books, 1999); Michael I. N. Dash, Jonathan Jackson, and Stephen C. Rasor, *Hidden Wholeness: An African American Spirituality for Individuals and Communities* (Cleveland: United Church Press, 1997); Marcia Y. Riggs, *Awake, Arise and Act: A Womanist Call for Black Liberation* (Cleveland: Pilgrim Press, 1994); Cheryl J. Sanders, *Empowerment Ethics for a Liberated People: A Path to African American Social Transformation* (Minneapolis: Fortress Press, 1995).

dimensions of survival and liberation referred to by Watkins Ali: recovery of self, recovery of culture and traditions, self-determination, and protection from and resistance against forces that would attempt to deny a people's sense of self and self-determination.

Identity in Joshua is also manifested in rituals that help persons remember who they are. Throughout the book of Joshua rituals of remembrance empower the people along their journey. One of the more significant rituals is the mass circumcision at Gilgal. Because there had been no circumcisions during the forty-year wandering in the wilderness, a whole generation of males failed to receive an important sign of their religious identity. So after crossing the Jordan, but before engaging in battle, Joshua arranges for the new generation of Israelites to be circumcised. In this ritual all the males who had been born in the wilderness are now incorporated into the people of the promise. Prior to this point they were not legitimate heirs of the promise; after circumcision they are. The ritual of circumcision secures not only their identity but also their rightful claim to their inheritance.

Joshua 5:10 recounts that the people of Israel kept the Passover in the plains of Jericho just prior to the siege of Jericho. The impression given is that remembering who they were was a crucial element in the victory at Jericho. Identity in Joshua is also addressed in the form of commitments and allegiance. When the Reubenites, Gadites, and half-tribe of Manasseh were returning to Transjordan, they built an altar on the Canaan side, which was interpreted by the rest of the Israelites as "in breach of faith toward the LORD"(22:22). In response the Reubenites, Gadites, and half-tribe of Manasseh explained that it was an altar of remembrance and dedication. They were anticipating a time when their children might one day be asked by the children of those on the other side of the Jordan, "What have you to do with the LORD, the God of Israel?"(22:24). The altar was meant to be a reminder that the Reubenites, Gadites, and Manassites did perform in service to the LORD and that there is a bond between the ancient Israelites on both sides of the Jordan. The altar was to become a witness through the generations to the shared identity that exists among the people of God.

In the last chapter Joshua gathers the people at Shechem. There he reviews the entire history of the Israelites, going back to their origins before Abraham. In this summary review Joshua reminds the people of the many victories God has accomplished on their behalf, ending with this statement:

> "Now therefore revere the LORD, and serve him in sincerity and in faithfulness; put away the gods that your ancestors served beyond the River and in Egypt, and serve the LORD. Now if you are unwilling to serve the LORD, choose this day whom you will serve, whether the gods your ancestors served in the region beyond the River or the gods of the Amorites in whose land you are living; but as for me and my household, we will serve the LORD." (24:14–15)

Once the people declare their allegiance to the God who through history has preserved them, Joshua presses them and asks if they are serious about this commitment to the Lord. They respond in the affirmative. Joshua then says, "You are witnesses against yourselves that you have chosen the LORD, to serve him" (24:22). At Shechem the people of God reaffirm that they are God's people and thereby solidify their identity through their promise to be faithful to God, who has been faithful to them.

The story of Rahab presents another perspective on the issue of identity in Joshua. Clearly Rahab is not part of the people encamped at Gilgal waiting to enter the promised land. She is already there, operating a family business. Although she is not a member of the twelve tribes, she becomes incorporated into the mission and identity of the ancient Israelites. When Joshua sends spies to reconnoiter the situation in Jericho, they reside in the house of Rahab, who is an inhabitant of Jericho. Rahab has heard of the Lord's deliverance of the Israelites from Egypt and believes that the Lord will follow through on the promise to deliver the promised land to them. In return for sparing her life and the lives of her family members when the invasion occurs, Rahab offers to hide the spies from the soldiers of the king of Jericho. The spies agree to this arrangement and instruct Joshua not to harm Rahab or her family when Jericho is taken. The Israelites honor their agreement with Rahab and spare her and her family. The rest of the inhabitants of Jericho are destroyed.

The narrative goes on to say that Rahab continued to dwell among the ancient Israelites, and in Matthew 1:5 Rahab is named in the genealogy of Jesus. Later, in Hebrews 11:31, she is described as a hero of the faith. So here we have Rahab, who is not a descendant of Abraham, who has not been a participant in the history of the people of God, who has not participated in the rituals of the Israelites, and who has not made a commitment of allegiance to God prior to the invasion. Yet she becomes a member of the ancient Israelites and is eventually lifted up as an example of faithfulness. In essence her identity is wrapped up in her role as an agent in the furthering of God's destiny for God's people.

In Joshua identity is associated with living within the destiny that God has proposed for God's people, engaging in rituals of remembrance of that destiny, and playing an active role in the actualization of that destiny.

Connectedness

There are numerous ways in which the African American community is fragmented and disconnected. Lincoln and Mamiya, drawing on the work of William Julius Wilson, describe class divisions within the African American community as one of the biggest challenges facing the black church in the future. The black middle class is growing larger, but at the same time blacks in poverty are growing in numbers, especially women and children. The gap between the two different groups is growing larger.

Orlando Patterson concludes that African American men and women are the most disconnected couples of all populations. The marriage rate between them is decreasing; that is, fewer and fewer African Americans are entering into marriage. The divorce rate among African Americans is on the rise. So we have a situation in which fewer blacks are getting married and those who are married are divorcing more frequently.

We have noted that Archie Smith speaks of spiritual refugees who have lost a depth of dimension, reflexivity, and agency, and that Edward Wimberly identifies relational refugees as a growing part of African American populace whose alienation from themselves and their communities has increased their vulnerability to emotional and spiritual disease. Father absence has been described as a chief contributor to African American family disruption and poverty among African American families.[15] Father absence from African American families is yet another aspect of disconnectedness within African American social structure. Given such challenges facing African Americans in their relations with one another, can the Joshua story provide any insights?

Joshua and Connectedness

Second to the promises of God to deliver the land, the success of the conquest of the promised land depended on the unity of the ancient Israelites. When unity faltered, the success of the campaign was put in jeopardy. The first example of committed relationship among the people of God in Joshua is found in the commitment that the Reubenites, Gadites, and half-tribe of Manasseh make to the conquest enterprise. Joshua reminds these tribes in Joshua 1 that the inheritance of their land in Transjordan depends on their assistance in the campaign across the Jordan. It might have been possible for the Transjordan tribes to claim the land they had settled in and refuse to join the rest of the Israelites in their claim of the inheritance. However, their sense of bond and connection to the rest of the tribes moved them to do battle in and for land that they were not to occupy. The Reubenites, Gadites, and Manassites had internalized an identity such that their individual interests were incorporated into the collective interests of all their people. This sense of connectedness led them to join with their brothers and sisters in an enterprise of survival and liberation from which they were not to benefit directly. Yet they joined with their brothers and sisters because they viewed themselves as participants in the larger claim of an inheritance that was promised to all of Abraham's heirs. For them there was no individual claim, only a collective claim.

---

[15] *Turning the Corner on Father Absence in Black America: A Statement from the Morehouse Conference on African American Fathers* (Atlanta: Morehouse Research Institute and Institute for American Values, 1999).

After their dramatic victory at Jericho, the Israelites are defeated in their campaign at Ai. The defeat at Ai recorded in Joshua 7 appears to negate the notion that God is on the side of the Israelites, guaranteeing them victory in the promised land. However, the defeat at Ai results not from God's failure to deliver but from the failure of Achan to be faithful to God. God had commanded that no spoils be taken for personal gain. Rather, whatever gold or silver was retrieved was to be devoted to the Lord. When Joshua inquires of God why they were defeated at Ai, God answers, "Israel has sinned; they have transgressed my covenant that I imposed on them; they have taken some of the devoted things; they have stolen, they have acted deceitfully, and they have put them among their own belongings" (7:11).

God directs Joshua to interrogate the people in order to determine who has broken the commandment and to punish them. Joshua then conducts the investigation and discovers that Achan has kept a mantle and some silver and gold. In punishment for his deceit Achan and his whole family are stoned to death and burned. Soon after the death of Achan and his family another attack is made on Ai that is successful because ancient Israel is again in faithful obedience to God. Here again, we have a rather gruesome story in Joshua, one that confronts us with a God who is ruthless in meting out punishment. Beneath the gruesome details of the story a principle exists related to the theme of connectedness. The interpreters of the *Revised Standard Version* of the Bible refer to this principle as a "unitary view of society."[16] In this unitary view of society what one member of a group does has ramifications for all members of that group. There is no individual action that does not have corporate consequences. In fact, the manner in which it is presented in Joshua suggests that the action of an individual is tantamount to being the action of the whole group. Chapter 7, verse 1 demonstrates this merger of individual and collective identity:

> But the *Israelites* broke faith in regard to the devoted things: *Achan* the son of Carmi son of Zabdi son of Zerah, of the tribe of Judah, took some of the devoted things; and the anger of the LORD burned against the *Israelites* [italics mine].

Achan's actions not only condemn him but implicate all his ancestors, all his tribe, and all Israel. This same perspective is echoed in 7:11 when God asserts that through the behavior of Achan all of Israel has sinned. The unitary view of society applies to the punishment for the action as well. Not only is Achan put to death but all his household as well, including his children and his animals. The story of

---

[16] *The Oxford Annotated Bible with the Apocrypha: Revised Standard Version* (New York: Oxford University Press, 1965), 270.

Achan within the story of Joshua reflects clearly the ancient perspective that one's individual identity and behavior were inextricably connected to that of one's cultural group.

Previously we examined the relationship between the two groups of Israelites who lived across the Jordan from each other under the topic of identity, but it can also be seen in terms of connectedness. The driving force behind the desire of the Reubenites, Gadites, and Manassites to occupy the land in Transjordan was the fact that the Transjordan land would better support their livelihood as raisers of cattle and sheep. That is why they had requested of Moses that they be allowed to settle in the Transjordan territory rather than in the land across the Jordan. Moses granted their request but demanded that they participate in the battles to be waged across the Jordan. The Reubenites, Gadites, and Manassites agreed: " 'As the LORD has spoken to your servants, so we will do. We will cross over armed before the LORD into the land of Canaan, but the possession of our inheritance shall remain with us on this side of the Jordan'" (Num. 32:31–32). A number of interpretations can be made of the participation of these peoples in the conquest of the promised land across the Jordan. One interpretation is that their participation was a "business arrangement." Moses had made a deal with them: They could have the Transjordan if they fought with their brothers and sisters across the Jordan; otherwise they would have to settle in Canaan with the rest of the tribes. Moses instructed Joshua and the other leaders:

> "If the Gadites and the Reubenites, everyone armed for battle before the LORD, will cross over the Jordan with you and the land shall be subdued before you, then you shall give them the land of Gilead for a possession; but if they will not cross over with you armed, they shall have possessions among you in the land of Canaan." (Num. 32:29–30)

The interpretation could be made that the Reubenites, Gadites, and Manassites helped in the conquest only to get what they wanted, that they did it only out of self-interest. Another interpretation for the motivation of the Transjordan tribes is that of fear. When the Reubenites, Gadites, and Manassites first approached Moses about settling in Transjordan, Moses responded with a scathing attack: "Shall your brothers go to war while you sit here? Why will you discourage the heart of the Israelites from going over into the land that the LORD has given to them?" (Num. 32:6–7). Moses goes on to link their perceived selfishness with the cowardliness of their ancestors who questioned whether or not the land could be possessed. God's anger was kindled by their lack of faith, and God made the people wander in the wilderness for forty years. Moses ends his scolding with the threat that if they do not help in the campaign, they will have sinned against the Lord, and the Lord will find them out. One could speculate that shame and fear instead of a sense of connectedness motivate the Reubenites, Gadites, and Manassites to join their brothers and sisters in battle.

However, the behavior of the Transjordan tribes just prior to going back over the Jordan after the campaign negates these other interpretations of motivation and reveals a genuine connectedness that the Transjordan tribes felt for their fellow Israelites. Having "earned" their inheritance by waging war, the Reubenites, Gadites, and Manassites could have just turned their backs, headed east, and severed their connection to those who were settled in Canaan. Instead, they built an altar of remembrance on the west side of the Jordan. This altar was to be a reminder to them and their children, as well as to the descendants of those in Canaan, that a bond exists between the two groups. On either side of the Jordan a true and authentic bond did exist that was not motivated by self-interest, shame, or fear. Rather, the Transjordan tribes saw themselves as connected to the Canaanite tribes and wished for that connection to survive throughout the generations. Their connection to one another was rooted in their connection with God, who had faithfully delivered on the promises to all of Israel.

Vision of the Future

The freedom movement among African Americans has always had guiding visions that directed its thoughts and actions. At times these visions conflicted with one another, but there never was an absence of vision. The current struggle for survival and liberation does not have the clarity of vision that has existed previously. African Americans today are vision starved. And what visions do exist either focus too much on the past rather than the future or lack compelling conviction to move a people forward. Although the Joshua story described a vision for a people on a journey of survival and liberation three thousand years ago, I believe parts of that vision have relevance for blacks today.

In the eighteenth century the vision of the future that blacks possessed was simply that of being perceived as human beings. It was a "limited" vision in that it did not include grand plans for freedom and liberation. Yet it was a "monumental" vision because being perceived as a human being was foundational to any consideration of the human and civil rights afforded to other humans at the time, such as life, liberty, and the pursuit of happiness.

Blacks who were literate at the time tried to demonstrate their humanity in a number of ways. First, they told their life stories. These autobiographies indicated that blacks, like whites, had life narratives and thereby lives full of the emotions, feelings, experiences, thoughts, and desires that were a part of any human life:

> For in *every* human Breast, God has implanted a Principle, which
> we call Love of Freedom; it is impatient of Oppression, and pants

for Deliverance; and by the leave of our modern Egyptians I will assert, *that the same Principle lives in us.*[17]

Moreover, the humanness of blacks was demonstrated by their capacity to think, write, feel, and learn. Blacks were not animals devoid of emotions, reason, or intellect. Rather, blacks had all the human capacities and capabilities of whites. Many of the authors had to verify that they had written their own works of art by adding the phrase "written by himself or herself" or having a panel of respected white authorities vouch for the writer's capacity to write what was produced.[18] In some cases the blacks attempted to prove their humanity through the adoption of practices and behavior of whites.[19] For eighteenth-century blacks a primary vision of the future was that blacks would be seen as human beings.

The validation of African American humanity was essential and foundational for the associated image of their vision: the elimination of slavery. Both Wheatley and Equiano included a denunciation of slavery and an appeal to eliminate it. Wheatley writes, "God grant Deliverance in his own Way and Time, and get him honour upon all those whose Avarice impels them to countenance and help toward the Calamities of their fellow Creatures."[20] Equiano writes even more boldly and graphically:

> O ye nominal Christians! Might not an African ask you, learned you this from your God, who says unto you, Do unto all men as you would men do unto you? Is it not enough that we are torn from our country and friends to toil for your luxury and lust of gain? Must every tender feeling be likewise sacrificed to your avarice? Are the dearest friends and relations, now rendered more dear by their separation from their kindred, still to be parted from one another, and thus to be prevented from cheering the gloom of slavery with the small comfort of being together and mingling their

---

[17]Phillis Wheatley, "To Samson Occom, February 11, 1774," in Julian D. Mason, ed., *The Poems of Phillis Wheatley* (Chapel Hill, N.C.: The University of North Carolina Press, 1989), 204 (italics mine).

[18]At the beginning of Phillis Wheatley's *Poems on Various Subjects, Religious and Moral,* the Preface included a letter sent by Wheatley's master to the publisher attesting to her capacities in the English language and Latin along with a statement by the Governor of Massachusetts and seventeen other dignitaries (including John Hancock) attesting to the fact that the poems were actually written by Wheatley. They produced this statement after having had an interview with Wheatley in which she had to demonstrate that she was capable of having written the poems. In 1789 Olaudah Equiano, a former slave, wrote an autobiography titled, "The Interesting Narrative of the Life of Olaudah Equiano, or Gustavus Vassa, the African, Written by Himself." It is in Henry Louis Gates, Jr., and Nellie Y. McKay, eds., *The Norton Anthology of African American Literature* (New York: W.W. Norton and Co., 1997), 138–64.

[19]See chapter 4 of Equiano's autobiography, found in the *Norton Anthology* on p. 164.

[20]Wheatley, "To Samson Occom," 204.

sufferings and sorrows? Why are parents to lose their children, brothers their sisters, or husbands their wives? Surely this is a new refinement in cruelty, which, while it has no advantage to atone for it, thus aggravates distress, and adds fresh horrors even to the wretchedness of slavery.[21]

Much African American literature in the pre–Civil War period reflected these dual themes of the abolition of slavery and the promotion of equal status for blacks. Whereas Wheatley and Equiano addressed their appeal to whites for the abolition of slavery and the promotion of equal status, David Walker appealed to blacks to begin the campaign to acquire these two goals. Walker's vision for the future for blacks was that they would acquire certain attributes and traits plus an identity that would counter the ravaging effects of slavery that had made African Americans "the most degraded, wretched, and abject set of beings that ever lived since the world began."[22] Walker asks:

Are we Men!!…are we Men? Did our Creator make us to be slaves to dust and ashes like ourselves?…Have we any other Master but Jesus Christ alone? Is he not their Master as well as ours? – What right then, have we to obey and call any other Master, but Himself? How we could be so submissive to a gang of men, whom we cannot tell whether they are as good as ourselves or not, I never could conceive.[23]

Walker's appeal seeks to rouse people to a violent struggle to unburden themselves from slavery. In doing so they should not fear their enemies and should take pleasure in being black. In Walker's vision for the future African Americans are a proactive people whose sense of pride in themselves moves them to defend themselves without fear from any efforts to degrade or enslave them. For Walker the future is a protracted war to recover dignity, self-determination, and freedom.

While Walker's question is "Are we Men?" Sojourner Truth's question is "Ain't I a woman?" This is the question she asked at the Women's Rights Convention in Akron, Ohio, in June 1851. In response to the challenge of equal rights for women posed by male ministers at the convention, Sojourner Truth's speech was a brilliant retort to both sexism and racism. One minister employed the image of women needing assistance from men to get into carriages and over ditches as an indication of women's limitations. He also accused women of the vanity of needing to be seated in the best place. He said these qualities about women showed their lack of fortitude and their

---

[21]Equiano, "The Interesting Narrative," 161.
[22]David Walker, "David Walker's Appeal," in *Norton Anthology,* 179.
[23]Ibid., 189.

inability to withstand the hardship and sacrifice required for full participation in the political realm.

Sojourner Truth, baring her arm, spoke to her own strength and experience of plowing, planting, and gathering, which was done without the help of a man and equaled the work effort of a man. Thus the question "Ain't I a woman?" countered the argument that women were less than men and supported the notion that in many ways women could compete equally with men. But in the course of her response Sojourner Truth also stated, "Nobody ever helped me into carriages, or over mud puddles, or given me any best place." This statement was followed by the question "and ain't I a woman?" Sojourner Truth was referring here not only to gender discrimination but racial discrimination as well. The fact that she had not been treated like other women was not based on the fact that she was not a woman but on the fact that she was black. From this perspective the question "and ain't I a woman?" carries with it a silent "also." Sojourner Truth is telling her audience, both male and female, that she is a victim of both sexism and racism.

What was Sojourner Truth's vision for the future? It was a vision of a society where all people—men, women, white, and black—would be given the opportunity to develop to the fullest of their potential. "Then they talk about this thing called intellect…What's that got to do with women's rights or niggers' rights? If my cup won't hold but a pint and yours holds a quart, wouldn't you be mean not to let me have my little half-measure full?"

In the nineteenth century, the vision for the future of African Americans had three dimensions: (1) blacks freed from slavery, (2) the development of inner qualities necessary for life as a free people, and (3) the transformation of America.

The push for blacks to take the initiative and fight for their freedom was taken up by Henry Highland Garnett. This African American Presbyterian minister encouraged slaves to confront their masters and demand to be freed. Garnett, who believed that it was better to die than be a slave, preceded Malcolm X when he directed blacks to fight for their freedom by any means necessary. "Neither God nor angels, or just men, command you to suffer for a single moment, therefore it is your solemn and imperative duty to use every means, both moral, intellectual, and physical, that promises success."[24] An alternative vision was presented by Maria Stewart. In her *Religion and the Pure Principles of Morality, the Sure Foundation on Which We Must Build,* this black political writer encouraged blacks to avoid killing, burning, or destroying, but "to improve your talents; let not one lie buried in the earth. Show forth your powers of mind. Prove to the world that "though black your skins as shades of night, your hearts are pure, your

---

[24]Henry Highland Garnett, "An Address to the Slaves of the United States of America," in *Norton Anthology,* 282.

souls are white."[25] Stewart believed that a people that made the most of their God-given talents would be recognized as worthy of freedom and self-determination.

James Whitfield's poem on self-reliance recommends yet another human attribute for African Americans to appropriate in order to defeat forces that attack the spirit and lead to despair: "I love the man whose lofty mind on God and its own strength relies; who seeks the welfare of his kind, and dare be honest though he dies." Here Whitfield is merging two apparent opposites: self-reliance and reliance on another. However, the theological argument that Whitfield is making is that the source of any power that a person possesses and relies on is from God. Self-reliance incorporates God-reliance. In Whitfield's vision for the future for African Americans, self-reliance, honesty (being true to one's self), and solidarity will contribute to the success of blacks in all future battles.

But trusting in the aid of Heaven,
And wielding with unfaltering arm,
The utmost power which God has given-
Conscious that the Almighty power
Will nerve the faithful soul with might,
Whatever storms might round him lower,
Strikes boldly for the true and right.[26]

While others before him had named the hypocrisy of America's claim of liberty and justice for all, Frederick Douglass made the incongruity between America's ideals and slavery a cornerstone of his message. "The existence of slavery in this country brands your republicanism as a sham, your humanity as a base pretense and your Christianity a lie."[27] In his vision for the future the fraud and deception of America are exposed and the country lives in harmony with its creeds: both African Americans *and* America are delivered from the bonds of slavery. Frances E.W. Harper presents a picture of the future if slavery does not end. Her antislavery poem "An Appeal to My Country Women" includes these lines:

Oh, people sin-laden and guilty,
So lusty and proud in your prime,
The sharp sickles of God's retribution
Will gather your harvest of crime.
Weep not, oh my well-sheltered sisters,
Weep not for the Negro alone,

[25]Maria W. Stewart, "Religion and the Pure Principles of Morality, the Sure Foundation on Which We Must Build," in *Norton Anthology,* 203.

[26]James M. Whitfield, "Self-Reliance," in *America and Other Poems* (Buffalo, N.Y.: James S. Leavitt, 1853).

[27]Frederick Douglass, "What to the Slave is the Fourth of July?" in *Norton Anthology,* 389.

But weep for your sons who must gather
The crops which their fathers have sown.[28]

Implied in Harper's apocalyptic vision is a countervision for America if it does eliminate the scourge of slavery from its midst. The blessings of a righteous nation will include freedom from fear, guilt, retribution, and woe.

During the period between Reconstruction and the New Negro Movement in the 1920s, three differing viewpoints on the future for African Americans began to appear. These differing viewpoints were sometimes in sharp conflict with one another and resulted in split allegiances within the African American community. One such conflict was that between Booker T. Washington and W. E. B. DuBois. Each man was committed to removing the veil that hindered black progress, but each had vastly different approaches to how the veil was to be lifted.[29] In Booker T. Washington's future blacks would eventually secure full equal rights with whites, but for the immediate future they needed to cast their bucket down where they were and make fewer political demands. Casting one's bucket down where you were meant casting one's lot with the South rather than migrating to the North and developing skills in agriculture and the trades rather than seeking professional careers.

DuBois, on the other hand, championed the belief that African Americans should be granted full civil rights immediately, whether that be in the South or the North. To lead the masses of black people out of the indentured servanthood they occupied after slavery, DuBois suggested that an elite cadre of black leaders be developed who would provide the leadership for the remaining populace of blacks. Washington's future vision had blacks making the most of the resources, location, and opportunities that were readily available. DuBois's vision of the future had blacks entering into those places where they had been denied access.

Not only were their visions different, each was working with a different timeline. For Washington the immediate development of agricultural and manual labor skills came first, with the acquisition of political power coming later. For DuBois any delay in the denial of political power and civil rights was an affront and needed to be addressed immediately. Unfortunately, both men and their followers perceived their differing views as mutually exclusive. The visions were different but not necessarily mutually exclusive. In the final analysis African Americans are in need of a comprehensive vision for the future that can address the complex situation of their lives.

The New Negro Movement or Harlem Renaissance of the 1920s contributed a new dimension to the survival/liberation movement of African

---

[28]Frances E. W. Harper, "An Appeal to My Country Women," in *Norton Anthology,* 423.

[29]The veil motif runs throughout DuBois's *The Souls of Black Folk,* and at Tuskegee University Booker T. Washington is depicted in a famous statue lifting a veil off a former slave who looks out with awe and anticipation.

Americans. Up until that time the life situation of blacks was seen as a problem associated with the external forces of enslavement and discrimination. The New Negro Movement proposed a vision for the future whose focus was much more internal than external. Alain Locke, the movement's most eloquent spokesman,[30] emphasized renewed self-respect and self-dependence. He encouraged blacks to enter into a new phase in which the focus was on common consciousness versus common conditions, a life in common versus a problem in common. With this new vision of the future blacks would celebrate the unique, authentic, and life-sustaining aspects of their culture. With a shared consciousness about being black and the acknowledgement of a shared life together, blacks could live with greater pride and self-determination. With this greater race consciousness blacks could assert a stronger claim on their contribution to American life.[31] Blacks no longer would feel constrained to hide their culture, language, and ways of looking at the world. Instead, blacks were encouraged to assert their blackness as a real and authentic part of their humanity.[32]

This new phase of race consciousness called for a new set of relationships between blacks and whites. No longer were black people to be seen as a problem or as a cause that produced only sentimentality for the plight of blacks. Locke and others castigated such pity and called for what he referred to as "real contact." Such real contact recognized the giftedness of black people and their culture. Real contact meant that blacks and whites interacted as equals without white condescension. Black people and their culture no longer had to meet white approval to find acceptance; rather, black people and their culture enjoyed a credibility and validity of their own. The heightened race consciousness led some not toward a greater desire to assert their blackness in America but to reject America as a place where racial pride and empowerment could exist. Thus, Marcus Garvey and the Universal Negro Improvement Association encouraged blacks to join with their African brothers and sisters in Liberia to create a place where Africans in diaspora and Africans on the continent could reunite as one people.

In 1940 Richard Wright did a sociological study of African Americans in Chicago. With camera and pen he recorded the conditions of African Americans in the black neighborhoods. What he found was that the large influx of blacks resulting from the great migration did not find a promised land. Rather, blacks found themselves living in poverty in cramped housing, confined to discrete sections of the city. The poignancy of these conditions

---

[30]Alain Locke, "The New Negro," in *Norton Anthology*, 961–70.
[31]Langston Hughes, "I, Too Am America," in *Norton Anthology*, 1258.
[32]Ibid., 1271.

pushed many in the black community to focus the vision for the future on the tragic conditions of blacks in the urban environment. Wright's book *Native Son* paints a graphic picture of the hardship and pathos of the black urban community in the middle of the twentieth century. Other writers, such as Ralph Ellison, James Baldwin, and Lorraine Hansberry, were not as hopeless and despairing about the black urban community. They believed that there were aspects of black culture and black family life that allowed blacks to transcend the grip of abject poverty and deplorable living conditions of the urban setting.

Integration as a vision for the future emerged as the answer for blacks in the mid-1950s. I will not discuss here in full the problems with the integration vision, for others have done extensive reviews of the limits of integration as a viable solution to the racial divide between blacks and whites in America. Suffice it to say here that integration's implied agenda that blacks forgo their black identity in order to appropriate a white identity and a racist society's refusal to acknowledge its racism have led to an abandonment of the integration agenda, especially as formulated in 1960s. The first attacks on the integrationist vision came from the black power movement and the black Muslims. Recently Dr. King's dream of little black boys and girls joining hands with little white boys and girls as sisters and brothers has been dealt a serious blow by the attacks on affirmative action, the Rodney King incident, and police racial profiling. Dr. King's question remains: "Where do we go from here?" Does the Joshua story provide any help in finding an answer to this question?

Joshua and a Vision for the Future

Prior to entering the promised land, the ancient Israelites' vision for the future was that of a land flowing with milk and honey. In the wilderness the idyllic picture they had of their future existence was that of settling into a place where all their needs would be met in an extravagant manner. Not only would there be no more wandering in the wilderness, wondering where food and water would come from, they would settle in a place where there would be an abundance of all the best things. However, after they crossed the Jordan, the idyllic image was no longer used to describe life in Canaan, present or future. Having engaged in hard-fought battles to claim the land that had been promised to them, the Israelites came to know a different way to understand their present and future destiny. Instead of perpetual peace and rest, life in Canaan would always be a struggle to survive and maintain freedom. The future would always be a battle to retain their identity, sustain their solidarity, and resist further oppression.

After the conquered land is divided among the tribes by Joshua in chapters 13–21, the final three chapters in Joshua describe a vision for the future of life in Canaan. Once the Transjordan tribes were released to settle across the Jordan, they realized that their identity as Israelites linked to the

Israelites on the eastern side of the Jordan was in jeopardy for the future. They could anticipate a time when their children might be asked what they had to do with the Lord God of Israel and the people of Israel. Their vision for the future included the desire for their children to be able to know and readily recite who they were and whose they were. The ancient Israelites also anticipated that separation among the people of God would necessarily erode some of that identification and cultural solidarity. Consequently, as we have seen, the Transjordan tribes built an altar on the Canaan side on their way back to Transjordan as a reminder to their children and a witness to God that there exists now and will exist in the future a connection between the two groups.

Black people in America are perpetually in diaspora. Moreover, this scatteredness across America is only matched by scatteredness across lines of class, viewpoints, skin color, and concepts of how to make black America better.[33] Lured by capitalistic gain, or escaping the fact that they are black, or confused by what it means to be black, blacks have lost touch with that which informs them of who they are. I propose the following statement as a vision for African Americans at this turn of the century: *We are God's people, created black, free, and embedded in a culture of rich texture and flavor, whose purpose is to make known the love, grace, and power of God. We are engaged in the process of claiming as God's black people the inheritance of full humanity that God has promised to us.* The Transjordan tribes carried within them a consciousness of who they were. It was this consciousness that was awakened and moved them as they approached the Jordan to build an altar of remembrance. One cannot help but wonder that the altar, built on the Canaan side, was to be a reminder not only to the people on the west side of the Jordan but also to those on the east side that they were one people, linked by their common deliverance by God, linked by their past commitments to one another, linked by a common history, and linked by their commitments for the future to remember themselves to one another.

In Joshua, as in much of the Bible, *remembering* has a double meaning. *Remembering* refers to memory and keeping things in mind, but it also has to do with "re-membering," putting things back together. The dispute between the tribes in chapter 22 of Joshua both presents an imperative that the people of God work at reconciliation among themselves and proposes a process for such reconciliation. Just as it is not acceptable for the Transjordan tribes to take action that appears to sever their ties with the rest of the Israelites, so, too, it is unacceptable for the Israelites in Canaan to write off the Transjordan tribes. Their mutual commitment to one another, which is rooted in their common commitment to God, requires that the

---

[33]Tavis Smiley, *How to Make Black America Better: Leading African Americans Speak Out* (New York: Doubleday, 2001).

Canaanite Israelites reach out to the Reubenites, Gadites, and half- tribe of Manasseh to understand the meaning of the altar. Differences of opinion and viewpoint will surely exist as a people work together at defining their future and fulfilling their destiny. However, those differences should not result in the diminishment of collective power or be worked out in ways that contribute to fragmentation and separation.

Israelites in Canaan were disturbed that the Transjordan tribes built what appeared to them to be an altar for burnt offerings and sacrifice. Because altars for burnt offerings and sacrifices to God were to be built in a central location, the Israelites in Canaan believed the Transjordan tribes were breaking covenant with God and with the rest of their people. Initially they were ready to make war on the perceived renegades. However, first they sent a delegation from Canaan to determine what the action of the Transjordan tribes meant. After the explanation, there no longer was enmity between the two groups, and their sense of cohesive identity was maintained.

In the history of African Americans there have always been conflicts between blacks about how best to respond to their life circumstance: violent revolt against slavery or submissive acceptance of one's fate; establish a home in America or return to Africa; seek political empowerment and civil rights through the leadership of a talented tenth or achieve ownership of land and self-subsistence through skilled labor and farming; integration versus black power. There is no one strategy that will win victory for African Americans. As was the case in the conquest of Canaan, a variety of tactics and strategies will need to be employed. At any given time and in any given situation a unique combination of strategies will have to be employed to secure the survival and liberation of blacks in America. The future success of these endeavors depends on the ability to work cooperatively and constructively toward those ends. This will require the investment of time, energy, and thought in a discernment process from which all perspectives in the African American community are sought. In the face of conflicting viewpoints the task is not to alienate and thereby fragment, but to more deeply seek understanding and ways of working together.

In Joshua the fulfillment of the vision for the future resided in faithful adherence to the rituals and practices of the faith. Ritual was associated with every victory recorded in Joshua. Rituals of remembrance played a significant role in the survival and liberation of the Israelites. We have already looked at the ritual practice of circumcision as an important element in restoring Israelite identity recorded in chapter 5 of Joshua. Also in chapter 5 is a reference to the ritual of Passover. In preparation for the conquest of the land and in keeping with their faith tradition the Israelites celebrated Passover. In this section of Joshua the Passover is more than the remembrance of God's deliverance in a former time; it is a prelude to the recovery of self-sufficiency and self-determination. The composer of Joshua links the Passover with the cessation of manna dropped from heaven and the beginning of the Israelites' feeding on the produce of the land:

> While the Israelites were camped in Gilgal they kept the passover in the evening on the fourteenth day of the month in the plains of Jericho. And on the day after the passover, on that very day, they ate the produce of the land, unleavened cakes and parched grain. The manna ceased on the day when they ate the produce of the land, and the Israelites no longer had manna; they ate the crops of the land of Canaan that year. (Josh. 5:10–12)

The Israelites had entered into a new phase of relationship with God and the land. By exercising the rituals of the past in this new place, they were exercising a claim on the land. They claimed the land by living out their rituals of identity and remembrance in this new location. It became theirs as they linked it to their traditions, their history, and their culture. In return the land claimed them. No longer were they guests in someone else's home to be fed by another. Rather, they were now in their own home, able to provide a meal for themselves from the resources of their own home. This change in relationship to the land is also reflective of a change in relationship to God. For the Israelites at this critical juncture in their conquest God was no longer the sole and exclusive determiner of their destiny. God had promised them the land, and the success of their conquest had been guaranteed, but the role of the Israelites in the conquest had changed.

A much more active and less passive role was required of them. Rather than waiting for manna to fall from heaven, the Israelites had to work the land for their food. It would no longer be given to them; they had to actively participate in the claim of their inheritance. And so the next chapter of Joshua begins the story of this more active role the ancient Israelites assumed in their continued struggle for survival and liberation. A number of sayings are attributed to the Bible that do not appear in scripture. One of them is, "The Lord helps those who help themselves." Although those exact words do not appear in scripture, the story of the cessation of manna comes close to reflecting the sentiments of that saying.

Blacks in America at the beginning of the twenty-first century are faced with challenges related to identity, connectedness, and a vision for the future. Using the Joshua conjuration as a guide, we can see that on the issue of black identity Joshua suggests that blacks must struggle with discerning and living within the destiny that God has proposed for them, engaging in rituals of remembrance of that destiny, and playing an active role in the actualization of that destiny. I have defined that destiny as living black and free and claiming the inheritance of full humanity that God has promised them. An essential ingredient in the realization of their destiny is that blacks live in solidarity with one another. According to Joshua such solidarity is marked by a collective commitment to one another that transcends individual interests. And the guiding vision for the future in which identity, destiny, and connectedness are fulfilled is a dynamic vision in which black people are engaged in an ongoing struggle to claim the inheritance promised to them through reliance on God and collective self-determination.

The black church is the prime institution within the black community to carry African Americans forward into the fulfillment of their destiny in this century. Rather than a Moses or a Joshua, the black church as a *Joshua church* is well positioned to lead African Americans into a promised land that can truly be called home. First and foremost the black church knows the biblical story of promise, will, and guarantee that is located in Joshua. The black church not only knows this story intellectually; it has lived the Joshua story in its care and nurture of God's people throughout the years. From its start in the brush at night during slavery, to its welcoming of migrants to the city during the great migration, to its frontline stance during the civil rights movement, the black church has continually fought for the survival and liberation of blacks in America. This tradition of faithful service to the gospel through witness to the deliverance of God's black people makes the black church a ready vehicle for entrance into the promised land.

The black church contributes to positive black identity in a variety of ways. As black people gather in their houses of worship each Sabbath and during the week, they affirm one another in the belief that they are indeed a part of God's good creation. Whatever the world may say Monday through Saturday, the church delivers God's good news that blacks are a people of worth and value. African Americans come to know that their worth and value are not dependent on how much money they have, where they work, what their skin color is, or whom they know. Rather, their worth and value are rooted in the black life that they have been given and in the faithful use that they have made of that life. Traditionally, through preaching, worship, education, church governance, fellowship, and prayer, the black church has strengthened a people's resolve to survive against all odds and to seek liberation whenever oppression rears its head.

The black church promotes black identity through its protest against any efforts to diminish the dignity of black people and detour them from their destiny. That protest can take many forms. One crucial way in which that protest is taking place is through the black church's increased efforts to stem the epidemic of HIV/AIDS in the black community. Fortunately the black church has moved beyond the moralism associated with HIV/AIDS and has begun to recognize that regardless of how one contracted the disease, it is a terrible way to die and it is disproportionately killing black folk. Prevention and treatment programs in black churches have begun rapidly to increase the reputation of the black church as a place of healing and comfort, a reputation that is beginning to replace the black churches' initial identification with HIV/AIDS as places of judgment and abandonment.

Protest has also begun to take shape in battling the newer and more subtle forms of racism in American society, such as racial profiling and voter disenfranchisement. The Fifteenth Amendment gave blacks the right to vote. But what is the right to vote worth if one's vote is not counted? In the 2000 presidential election one out of every six votes for president in the black communities of Chicago was invalidated, mostly becaue of the poor condition of the voting machines. Black churches in Chicago and around the country are beginning to fight for voting reform that assists blacks in recovering what was formally guaranteed to them: one person, one vote. Through these protest efforts the black church mirrors the Joshua themes of recovery of its heritage and claiming of its inheritance, both for its people and for itself.

Many have written about the black church as a family or the black church as a family of families. What these writers are saying is that within the black church is a racial identity factor that transcends blood connection. Everyone is a brother or sister to one another. This kind of collective consanguinity is reflective of the kind of connectedness referred to in Joshua. It is the kind of connectedness that blacks in the twenty-first century will need in order to survive and fight the newer forms of oppression. To remain connected as a people is a battle in and of itself. Increased social and economic pressures for families to live farther apart from one another is one general feature of American life that impacts African Americans. But there are specific stressors placed on African Americans as they try to remain a connected and cohesive people.

That 20 percent of all African American males are incarcerated contributes to the difficulty in remaining connected as families and as a people. The growing gap between the classes of African Americans is also a source of deep concern for how a people remain connected. The distressing numbers associated with black divorce, single parenthood, and those never married suggest that more and more African Americans are choosing to live apart from one another rather than with one another. The black church as family has a legacy of keeping a people together in order to weather the storms of discrimination and oppression. That legacy of fostering a people's connectedness is one that the black church needs to appropriate even more than in the past.

In the past, segregation naturally kept African Americans together as a people. Not fully free to live, buy, ride, worship, and work wherever blacks wanted, we were more closely bound together as a people. The freedom of mobility accorded through civil rights victories gave blacks the benefit of greater social mobility and increased economic options but also severely cut at the bonds that kept blacks connected to one another. The results have been tragic. Pastoral theologians such as Wimberly and Butler are speaking to the growing sense of disconnectedness and isolation in the African American community. The black church as a place of gathering and as a place where persons can find acceptance and love is sorely needed at this time. The ministry tasks are clear: premarital counseling, couple and family counseling, conflict resolution, preaching that focuses on valuing one another, and the establishment of congregational atmospheres that are accepting, warm, and loving go a long way toward making persons feel that they have a home.

More than anything else the black church has been a generator of alternative visions of reality. Conjuring stories from the Bible and drawing on African folklore and myths, the black church has been able to transport black people from the oppression of the present moment to places of hope and deliverance. In the face of multiple visions for the future, some of which conflict with one another, can the black church help African Americans create a vision for the future that appreciates the complexity of various options and yet is true to the destiny God has in store for African Americans? With the weight of its moral and ethical calling, the rich resources of its tradition to do theology, and its significant historical role in the survival and liberation of blacks, the black church is uniquely qualified to lead a people out of the current wilderness of despair into the promised land of a fuller and more abundant life. In the twenty-first century the movement into the promised land will entail much in the way of recovery of a prideful identity and ritual to foster a sense of connectedness. When recovery and ritual are conducted in relationship with the God whose promise of inheritance carries with it the will and guarantee of victory, nothing will be able to impede the acquisition of a place where African Americans can live black, free, and in line with their destiny.

CHAPTER 3

Discerning Black Identity

The survival and liberation of blacks in the future depend on their successful struggle with the issues of cultural identity, connectedness, and vision. The loss of a cultural identity, the demise of a sense of connectedness, and the absence of a vision for the future jeopardize a people's capacity to determine a new and better life for themselves. On the other hand, a cohesive cultural identity, a felt solidarity, and a commitment to a shared vision for the future help to guarantee that a people will together find a common home of fulfillment and hope.

These issues of cultural identity, connectedness, and vision are very much interrelated. The cultural identity of black people in the future will be in large part determined by their connectedness to one another and their sense of vision for the future. Connectedness has much to do with whom one identifies with and whether a shared a vision is held. The integrity of a vision for the future depends on the trajectory established by cultural identity formation and the consistency of commitment over time. In this chapter we turn to the question of black identity and the inquiry that has emerged recently in the black community about what it means for a people to have a black cultural identity. The question of what constitutes a black cultural identity does not cover all the identity issues associated with recovery of a sense of self and cultural heritage. However, the question of what black cultural identity is forms the framework in which we will discuss the identity question.

A collective cultural identity assists a people in their efforts to remain connected and secure a vision for the future. But what is meant by a "collective" cultural identity? Is there an essential element that all black people have that, when claimed, denotes one as black, or black enough? Does it mean that there is a "litmus test" that all blacks must pass in order to be considered "black"? And if there is such a litmus test, what are the measurement criteria? Is it a question of skin color, or mannerisms, or political party? My answer to all these questions is no.

Black Essentialism

In chapter 1, I argued that African Americans should claim a collective cultural identity as a way of strengthening their campaign to survive and live out their destiny of full humanity. However, a sense of collective cultural identity should never be employed to exclude, shame, ridicule, or limit individuals within the collective. Cultural critics such as Randall Kenan, Victor Anderson, and Anthony Pinn have challenged the concept of black essentialism that is associated with the notion of a collective black cultural identity precisely because of its potential to exclude and limit individuals within the collective. For them black essentialism does not promote full humanity; rather, black essentialism limits the fulfillment of African Americans. In their search for a viable future for African Americans these thinkers have mounted a campaign to eradicate black essentialism.

Black essentialism, or racial essentialism for blacks, has been defined in a number of different ways. My understanding is that black essentialism is the belief that there is a core essence to black culture that is found in authentic expressions of black culture. In its role as definer of black cultural identity, black essentialism functions as a standard with which one can determine what is reflective of black culture and what is not. In its most positive use black essentialism functions to guide African Americans in perceiving what in black culture is true to the history and traditions of black people, as wells as to counter inaccurate stereotypes. In this vein Michael Eric Dyson has defined racial essentialism as "black intellectuals oppos[ing] the strangling of black culture by caricature, offering instead cultural standards to help define racial authenticity."[1] At its worst black essentialism acts as a screening device within the black community to judge who or what is truly black. Anderson refers to black essentialism as ontological blackness, viewing ontological blackness as the cult of black heroic genius.[2] "I use the word *cult* here to designate dispositions of devotion, loyalty, and admiration for racial categories and the essentialized principles

---

[1]Michael Eric Dyson quoted by Randall Kenan in *Walking on Water: Black American Lives at the Turn of the Twenty-First Century* (New York: Knopf, 1999), 9.

[2]Victor Anderson, *Beyond Ontological Blackness: An Essay on African American Religious and Cultural Criticism* (New York: Continuum, 1995), 13.

that determine black identity."[3] According to Anderson and others,[4] black essentialism grows out of an apologetic defense against the negative evaluation of blacks as a people.

As we have seen, this form of apologetics has a long history in the African American experience. Beginning with Phillis Wheatley and Oldaudah Equiano blacks have engaged in an ongoing battle to prove their humanity and to combat negative stereotypes. In the nineteenth century the apologetics took on a "genius" tone in which the unique nature of the African American was lifted up for praise and admiration. W. E. B Dubois's *The Souls of Black Folk* is a preeminent example. The argument was that inherent in the souls of black people are unique and special attributes that have enabled African Americans to survive the brutality of slavery and make significant contributions to the culture of North America. In the twentieth century these apologetics appeared in the literature, art, and music of the Harlem Renaissance, which argued that a distinctive African American cultural expression existed that did not copy the prevailing North American styles of popular culture. Later, in the political arena, African American apologetics fought for equality in all aspects of American society, especially civil rights. The belief was that blacks had a unique role to play in encouraging America to travel on the moral high ground of civil rights for blacks, thereby transforming America so that it reflected the ideals of freedom and justice it espoused. Black essentialism possesses a uniqueness, a power, and a genius that sets black people apart as a noble and proud people.

Detractors of black essentialism associate an ancillary problem with racial apologetics and its defense against categorical racism: black essentialism does not accurately examine the whole of African American cultural identity. The cult of black heroic genius tends to evaluate blacks and black culture with an excessively high regard. Almost everything about black people and their culture is regarded as better, optimal. A prime example of the optimal manner in which blackness can be viewed is in the work of Linda Myers.[5] Myers conceives of a black worldview that underlies black life and culture. This optimal black worldview stands over against a European/Western worldview that is less than optimal (see chart on page 74). Anderson and his associates would argue that such categorizations are

---

[3]Ibid.

[4]Darlene Clark Hine, "In the Kingdom of Culture: Black Women and the Intersection of Race, Gender, and Class," in *Lure and Loathing: Twenty Black Intellectuals Address W. E. B. Du Bois' Dilemma of the Double-Consciousness of African Americans,* ed. Gerald Early (New York: Penguin Group, 337–51); and Wilson J. Moses, "Ambivalent Maybe," in *Lure and Loathing,* 274–90.

[5]Linda Myers, *Understanding an Afrocentric World View: Introduction to Optimal Psychology* (Dubuque, Iowa: Kendall/Hunt Publishers, 1993).

too limited in their binary structure, do not allow for differentiation within categories, and do not allow for the less-than-optimal within black identity.

Ontological blackness is a philosophy of racial consciousness. It is governed by the dialectical matrices that existentially structure African Americans' self-conscious perceptions of black life. Under ontological blackness, the conscious lives of blacks are experienced as bound by unresolved binary dialectics of slavery and freedom,

CONCEPTUAL SYSTEMS		
Assumptions	**Optimal**	**Suboptimal**
Ontology (nature of reality)	Spiritual (known in an extrasensory fashion) and material (known through the five senses) as one	Material with possible spiritual aspect that is separate and secondary
Epistemology (nature of knowledge)	Self-knowledge known through symbolic imagery and rhythm	External knowledge known through counting and measuring
Axiology (nature of value)	Highest value in positive interpersonal relationships among people	Highest value in objects or acquisition of objects
Logic (reason)	Diunital—emphasizes union of opposites (both/and conclusions)	Dichotomous—emphasizes duality (either/or conclusions)
Process	Ntuology—all sets are interrelated through human and spiritual networks	Technology—all sets are repeatable and reproducible
Identity	Extended self, multi-dimensional	Individual form
Self-worth	Intrinsic in being	Based on external criteria or materialism
Values guiding behavior	Spiritualism, oneness with nature communalism	Materialism, competition, individualism
Sense of well-being	Positively consistent despite appearances due to relationship with source	In constant flux and struggle
Life—space	Infinite and unlimited (spirit manifesting)	Finite and limited (beginning with birth and ending with death)

negro and citizen, insider and outsider, black and white, struggle and survival. However, such binary polarities admit no possibility of transcendence or mediation.[6]

From Anderson's perspective, to be under ontological blackness is to be under a kind of slavery that provides no possibility for freedom or liberation; it is a permanent enslavement to ideals that offer no hope for something different.

The Quest to Move Beyond Ontological Blackness

In urging for a new cultural politics of difference that moves beyond ontological blackness, Anderson recommends that black life allow for individuality and differentness among African Americans, including the acknowledgment of the grotesque within the African American community. Rather than force all African Americans into a common box labeled "ontological blackness," African Americans should be seen as the diverse set of individuals that they are. If African Americans can free themselves from the cult of black heroic genius, they can release themselves from the fruitless enterprise of racial apologetics, live unfettered from the limiting vision of binary structures, no longer be blind to the less than heroic genius in their midst, and be free to live out their unique individual lives. Anderson calls such a life lived beyond ontological blackness a life lived in cultural fulfillment:

> Cultural fulfillment is the reflexive integration of basic human needs and subjective goods. It involves the satisfaction of categorical goods that human beings minimally require for maintaining biological life (life, safety, work, leisure, knowledge, and the like). It also involves the satisfaction of subjective goods (friendship, peace of mind, integrity of conscience, and spiritual meaning) that individuals require for alleviating subjective alienation, assuring subjective equilibrium and realizing positive personalities. Fulfillment of such needs and goods motivates the cultural activities of persons within society.[7]

Anderson and his colleagues are especially critical of the Black Theology Project, which they view as representative of ontological blackness's excursion into the realm of black religion. He concludes:

> Black theology constructs its new being on the dialectical structures that categorical racism and white racial ideology bequeathed to African American intellectuals (notwithstanding its claims for privileging black sources). However, the new being of black

---

[6]Anderson, *Beyond Ontological Blackness,* 14.
[7]Ibid., 49.

theology remains an alienated being whose mode of existence is determined by crisis, struggle, resistance, and survival—not thriving, flourishing, or fulfillment. Its self-identity is always bound by white racism and the culture of survival. The motive of transcendence from this unresolved matrix of struggle and survival recedes into the background as oppression is required for the self-disclosure of the oppressed. I suggest that as long as black theology remains determined by ontological blackness, it remains not only a crisis theology but also a theology in a crisis of legitimization.[8]

Anderson's critique of black theology follows the same critical line of thinking about ontological blackness. Although the apologetics of black theology takes a different tack than the apologetics of earlier black thinkers, the apologetic strain is still present. Earlier apologetics responded to the negative categorization of African Americans with arguments that justified the humanity and equal status of blacks. Black theology did not seek to justify the humanity and equal status of blacks (the humanity and equal status were assumed) but sought to give credence to the belief that God was on the side of the liberation struggle of African Americans and that there was theological justification for such a view. However, apologetic features still existed in black theology. First, black theology was a response to categorical racism and white racial ideology. Black theology challenged the prevailing theological thought at the time that ignored the existential situation of oppressed peoples. Black theology was a response to that silence and ignoring. The response was cast in a binary structure in which black theology stood over against white theology as its antithesis. With these apologetic and binary elements black theology fit within an ontological blackness framework.

One can sense the hegemonic, exclusionary, and universalizing clutch from which the critics of ontological blackness are trying to free themselves in the following statement from Joseph Washington:

> In the beginning was the black church, and the black church was with the black community, and the black church was the black community. The black church was in the beginning with the black people; all things were made through the black church, and without the black church was not anything made that was made. In the black church was life; and the life was the light of the black people.[9]

Anthony Pinn, another critic of ontological blackness, challenges what he perceives to be black theology's hegemonic enterprise to speak for all of the African American religious experience:

---

[8]Ibid., 87.

[9]Joseph Washington, "How Black Is Black Religion?" in *Quest for a Black Theology* (Maryknoll, N.Y.: Orbis Books, 1993), 5.

My view is that Christianity, its concept of God, humanity, and Christ, when construed as the normative expression of African American religion limits the relevance and truth content of other religious experiences that are not in keeping with church activity and doctrines. In short, to hold that Christianity is normative in theological conversation and methodological formulation of African American experience is to make its principles hegemonic or closed to discourse...their (Black Theology's) efforts are limited to the Christian context and apologies for the liberative content of the Gospel message, and varieties of faith existing outside of this context are excluded. [10]

Pinn argues for a pragmatic reconstruction of African American theology that is open to the variety of religious expressions found in the African American community. He helpfully presents this in *Varieties of African American Religious Experience.*[11] In this text he describes the religions of Voodoo, Yoruba, Islam, and Black Humanism with a discussion of their differing perspectives on the question of evil. Pinn's project is both a follow-up on Charles Long's[12] recommendation that the African American religious experience in America be examined in its totality and his own contribution to the cultural politics of difference.

Critique of Black Theology

Anderson and Pinn are particularly critical of the work of James Cone. Anderson views Cone's black theology as primarily responsive to white racism. Although the radical black consciousness that resides in black theology seeks to thwart the ravages of white racism on blacks and promote black survival, black theology conforms to the binary structure of black and white and is rooted in a heroic survivalist agenda. Anderson cites the following words from Cone to support his thesis:

The black experience is catching the spirit of blackness and loving it. It is hearing black preachers speak of God's love in spite of the filthy ghetto, and black congregations responding Amen, which means that they realize that ghetto existence is not the result of divine decree but of white inhumanity.[13]

---

[10]Anthony B. Pinn, "Rethinking the Nature and Tasks of African American Theology: A Pragmatic Perspective," *American Journal of Theology and Philosophy* 9 no. 2 (May 1998): 192–93.

[11]Anthony B. Pinn, *Varieties of African American Religious Experience* (Minneapolis: Fortress Press, 1998).

[12]Charles H. Long, *Significations: Signs, Symbols, and Images in the Interpretation of Religion* (Philadelphia: Fortress Press, 1986).

[13]James H. Cone, *A Black Theology of Liberation* (Maryknoll, N.Y.: Orbis Books, 1991), 25.

[The black experience] means having natural hair cuts, wearing African dashikis, and dancing to the sound of Johnny Lee Hooker or B.B. King, knowing that no matter how hard whitey tries there can be no real duplication of black "soul." Black soul is not learned; it comes from the totality of black experience, the experience of carving out an existence in a society that says you do not belong.[14]

For Anderson the black theology of Cone is problematic for a number of reasons. First, its ontological blackness is not ontological, because it requires whiteness, white racism, and white theology to justify its opposition to whiteness. Second, black theology speaks exclusively to the experience of suffering, survival, and resistance. Black theology, then, does not appear to have a transcendent dimension. Black existence from the ontological blackness perspective of black theology focuses on struggle and fails to address realities related to flourishing, thriving, and fulfillment. Anderson's complaints about the earlier work of the Black Theology Project also applies to its most recent proponents.

Anderson and Pinn describe the work of Dwight Hopkins, James Evans, and womanist theologians such as Katie Cannon, Delores Williams, Cheryl Sanders, and Marcia Riggs as falling under the rubric of the hermeneutics of return. These theologians refer to the ritual practices, cultural heritage, and organizational structures of the African American past in order to inform theological reflection on contemporary black life. For example, Dwight Hopkins has retrieved the folk religion, stories, rituals, and experiences of slaves participating in the "invisible institution" of slave religion to contribute to the enhancement of a constructive black theology.[15] In the invisible institution the foundation of a faith that has sustained black people in America over two hundred fifty years was born. To identify and clarify the features of that foundational faith make them more readily available for use in the present.

James Evans seeks "to articulate, interpret, and assess the essential doctrinal affirmations of African American faith for the contemporary African-American community of faith."[16] Cheryl Sanders and Marcia Riggs focus on the bifurcation within the black community between those who have achieved some modicum of empowerment and those who still languish in poverty and disadvantage. Drawing on the life and work of individual women of faith and women's groups, clubs, and organizations, Sanders and Riggs propose that the next phase of the liberation struggle must

---

[14]Ibid.

[15]Dwight N. Hopkins, *Shoes That Fit Our Feet: Sources for a Constructive Black Theology* (Maryknoll, N.Y.: Orbis Books, 1993) and *Down, Up, and Over: Slave Religion and Black Theology* (Minneapolis: Fortress Press, 1999).

[16]James H. Evans, Jr., *We Have Been Believers: An African-American Systematic Theology* (Minneapolis: Fortress Press, 1992), 6.

emphasize the ethical dimension of intragroup responsibility. Anderson and Pinn see the work of these latest black theologians as situated in the camp of ontological blackness. Their theologies are still concerned with struggle, survival, and resistance; they imply an essentialism that resides in African Americans across time, seek to recover a heroic genius found in the past, and fail to speak to an African American subjectivity that recognizes difference. Anderson designates these latest black theologies as operating within a hermeneutics of return. Even though they add another dimension to the Black Theology Project, they remain rooted in a racial apologetics enterprise.

While characterizing proponents of ontological blackness as stuck in the hermeneutics of return, advocates of a new cultural politics of difference for African Americans view themselves as participants in the more forward thrust of postmodernity. Indeed, the movement beyond ontological blackness is in part driven by its participation in the larger postmodern project. At its heart the postmodern project seeks to dismantle the hegemony that Western thought has had on defining the reality of human life and existence. Claiming a rational objectivity that rose above subjective opinions, modern Western thinkers, beginning with the Enlightenment, believed that they could eliminate any subjective bias from their observations and thereby achieve an uncompromised perspective on the truth. Postmodern thought has successfully challenged the claims of modern Western thought, arguing that any and all claims to absolute truth and objectivity are false. There is a subjective element in all truth claims, because every truth claim emerges from a worldview that has been shaped by a particular set of observations, experiences, and ways of making meaning often associated with one's culture or social location. As Clifford Geertz observed, all knowledge is local knowledge; that is, it is the product of a particular place, time, and person no matter how universalizing the thought or knowledge claims.[17] Postmodern thinkers, then, have "deconstructed" modern Western thought and robbed it of its hegemonic claim on the truth. Deconstructed Western thought has now been "decentered," making space for other worldviews and perspectives. A deconstructed and decentered worldview allows many more voices to be heard at the center of the debate about the reality and truth of things, and it acknowledges the differences that exist in these various perspectives. The task of Western thinkers in the modern paradigm was to determine whose truth and reality was worthy of occupying the hegemonic center. The postmodern task is to make sure that the whole variety of voices that could occupy the center are present and to avoid any one voice's claiming superiority or privilege.

---

[17]Clifford Geertz, *Local Knowledge: Further Essays in Interpretive Anthropology* (New York: Basic Books, 1983).

One can see in the work of those who seek to move beyond ontological blackness active participation in the postmodern project. Rather than have black identity be defined by the possession of an essential blackness, those in the cult of the cultural politics of difference for African Americans want to remove essential blackness from the center of black identity and replace it with the multitudinous ways in which blacks live out their blackness. The interest is not in sameness or essence but in variety and difference. And any attempt to impose a hegemonic definition of what it means to be black is viewed as a violation of the individual black person's difference *and* a blocking of that person's fulfillment.

Critical Perspective on a Black Cultural Politics of Difference

Although I have serious reservations about a cultural politics of difference for African Americans or black cultural politics of difference, there is much that I support in its effort to further the survival and liberation of African Americans. African Americans need no longer be apologetic about themselves. The old apologetics that argued for equal status as human beings and emancipation from slavery is certainly unnecessary. In addition, the newer apologetics that seeks to sustain the freedom movement and meet new challenges of racial categorization has adopted some problematic excesses.An emphasis on the black church must surely come across as alienating and offensive to African Americans whose faith is not Christian. Moreover, attempts to increase black self-esteem by positing that black worldviews are optimal, whereas Western European worldviews are suboptimal, do not allow for a thorough critical evaluation of either worldview. Is it really the case that there is nothing less than optimal about the black worldview? On what basis can African Americans make that claim? Daily assaults on the black psyche by the dominant society call for defensive strategies; but is the valorization of blacks that presents them as better than they are of service to blacks in the long run? Blacks run the risk of failing to view themselves and their circumstances realistically and thereby set themselves up for inevitable failure and disappointment.

Operating in the realm of essential blackness also carries the danger of excluding persons from participation in the collective effort for survival and liberation. When essential blackness is used as a litmus test for what it means to be black, it is quite easy to move into the unhelpful enterprise of figuring out who is black enough. Moreover, if essential blackness means possessing certain traits deemed inside or outside black culture, then blacks can easily fall into the trap of intraracial categorization, which bifurcates the community and leads to alienation. The freedom struggle needs every black person. To exclude any black because he or she is different from what is considered acceptable or in concert with essential blackness is to weaken the potential strength to be found in full participation by all blacks.

Black survival and liberation cannot afford to exclude participants because they are somehow different from a normative essential blackness.

An underlying theme to the beyond-ontological-blackness movement's critique of racial apologetics is crucial to the black struggle for survival and liberation. Apologetics is always responsive; that is, apologetics is always a response to a comment or action of another. Therefore, the agenda for the conversation or the course of action has been set by the initiator. The responder is locked into the agenda of the initiator and must relinquish a certain amount of agency and freedom in responding. On the one hand the response posture can be an effective way of disarming the initiator. Without a response there can be any number of negative outcomes for the nonresponder that could have been countered with an effective response. However, unless there is some initiative taken by the responder to set the agenda for the conversation or to determine the course of action, the responder is always at the mercy of the initiator for direction. Those in the new black cultural politics of difference movement point to this problem as a major shortcoming of racial apologetics within ontological blackness. Their question is, "Can there be a black cultural politics of difference that is not held captive to response to white racial categorization?" They seek a black cultural politics of difference where the task is not always to respond within a binary framework justifying essential blackness but rather to engage in the celebration of difference within the African American community that, hopefully, can be part of the larger celebration of difference within humankind.

The Realities of Suffering, Struggle, and Survival

Although the idealism of the black cultural politics of difference is very appealing, it does not address major issues related to the survival and liberation of African American people. As much as one would wish that it were not the case, racism is alive and well in North American society. It would be wonderful if African Americans could ignore the overt and subtle indignities blacks suffer at the hands of a culture dominated by white privilege. But if they did, they would do so at their peril. I, too, would like to pour all my energy into celebrating the variety of ways in which African Americans are achieving their fulfillment. If I did not have to concern myself with all the roadblocks, hurdles, gates, and ambushes along the way, that would be great. But the reality is that blacks are being murdered, lynched, infected, and failing to thrive in any number of different ways, as indicated in the Introduction. The cult of black cultural politics of difference fails to speak to these realities within the African American experience.

Yes, there must be attention given to fulfillment. But the attention to fulfillment must not be done at the expense of dealing with the realities of black suffering, struggle, and survival. Striving for fulfillment without paying attention to these other challenges will eventually undermine any possible fulfillment. If African Americans do not survive, they will not be able to achieve fulfillment. Now perhaps those who champion moving beyond ontological blackness believe that commitment to the goal of fulfillment will necessarily address the questions of suffering, struggle, and survival, but I am not convinced. Fulfillment assumes survival and emerges from it. Fulfillment does not work at survival but depends on it as a ground from which to work. At the point that survival is in jeopardy, fulfillment is suspended in order to work at survival. Although some forms of fulfillment that have arisen out of the struggle for survival, the task at hand was survival, not fulfillment.[18] In keeping with their own argument, the cult of black cultural politics of difference should not pit survival over against fulfillment in a binary structure that presents them as an either/or. Rather, survival (struggle, resistance) should be seen as accompanying fulfillment on the journey toward full humanity.

Genius and the Grotesque

In an effort to counter the excessive and unrealistic image of blacks as heroic geniuses, opponents of ontological blackness have introduced the concept of the grotesque as a counterbalance. The idea of genius that has developed in the West has often been seen as dialectically opposed to concepts such as talent, originality, and individuality.

> Evident in the history of the idea of genius is that the idea itself achieves a dialectical standing in relation to any number of other aesthetic categories: genius versus talent, genius versus taste, genius versus imitation. But the dialectics of genius comes to signify the opposition to originality, individuality, invention, inspiration, creativity in art, music, philosophy, and politics over tradition, gilded arts, mimesis, discovery, talent, and taste.[19]

The concept of grotesque seeks to remedy the distortions of genius not as an opposition between sensibilities, such as attraction and repulsion or pleasure and pain, but as an aesthetic device that leaves opposing sensibilities

---

[18]See Viktor Frankl, *Man's Search for Meaning: An Introduction to Logotherapy* (New York: Simon and Schuster, 1984); Bruno Bettleheim, *Surviving* (New York: Random House, 1979); B. A. Botkin's editing of slave narratives in *Lay My Burden Down: A Folk History of Slavery* (Chicago: University of Chicago Press, 1937); the slave narratives reported in Hopkins, *Down, Up, and Over* (New York: Knopf, 1979); Albert J. Raboteau, *Slave Religion: The "Invisible Institution" in the Antebellum South* (New York: Oxford University Press, 1980); or Cornel West, *Prophesy Deliverance: An Afro-American Revolutionary Christianity* (Philadelphia: Westminster Press, 1982). In all these works the authors discuss how persons were eking out an existence in order to survive, which then resulted in meanings, purposes, and opportunities for fulfillment.

[19]Anderson, *Beyond Ontological Blackness*, 122.

in tension with one another without negation or mediation. The presence of the grotesque allows for a full and accurate picture that does not favor one sensibility over the other. With a grotesque perspective we see both the good and the bad, the beautiful and the ugly, the heroic and the cowardly, the genius and the simple. Opponents to the cult of heroic genius argue that racial apologetics does not allow for the grotesque. Instead, it presents a picture of black life and culture that is skewed toward the noble and heroic. The grotesque perspective does not deny the noble and heroic, but it would place alongside it that which is less than noble, less than heroic, less than genius. This understanding of the grotesque supports the cult of black cultural politics of difference in its desire to present a picture of black life and culture that is multitudinous in its representation. Such a multitudinous representation would reflect all the variety and difference that exists in the African American community.

As a philosophical concept intended to correct the excesses of ontological blackness, the idea of a grotesque aesthetic makes some sense. However, the language of the grotesque is less than appealing for blacks and has the potential to reinforce white racial categorization of blacks as "less than." The popular understanding of the word *grotesque* connotes distortion and repulsion, but that popular understanding is not what Anderson is promoting. Borrowing from the work of Nietzsche, Thomson, and Burwick,[20] in which the grotesque receives a more neutral and in some cases benign treatment, Anderson proposes appropriation of the grotesque as a helpful device in countering the distortions of the cult of black heroic genius. Might not there be a different way of talking about this corrective without employing the language and image of the grotesque? For too long and too recently African Americans have been characterized in derogatory images associated with all that is ugly, deficient, and abnormal.[21] The concept of the grotesque, no matter how well explained or rationalized, will not be readily incorporated into the African American struggle for a fulfilled cultural identity.

The Promise of Postmodernity?

What is the nature of the relationship between postmodernity and the cult of a black cultural politics of difference? Is a new black cultural politics of difference an offshoot of the larger postmodern enterprise, or are postmodern sentiments employed by the new black cultural politics of

---

[20]Friedrich Nietzsche, *The Birth of Tragedy* (Garden City, N.Y.: Doubleday, 1956), *The Gay Science* (New York: Vintage Books, 1974), and *Twilight of the Idols* (New York: Penguin Books, 1990); Philip Thomson, *The Grotesque* (London: Methuen, 1972); Frederich Burwick, "The Grotesque: Illusion versus Delusion," in *Aesthetic Illusion: Theoretical and Historical Approaches,* ed. Frederick Burwick and Walter Pape (Berlin: de Gruyter, 1990), 122–37.

[21]Robert E. Hood, *Begrimed and Black: Christian Traditions on Blacks and Blackness* (Minneapolis: Fortress Press, 1994).

difference? That is, who is subject to whom? Or asked another way, how closely does the African American community want to align itself with the postmodern movement? David Daniels, my colleague at McCormick, has defined postmodernity in the following manner, albeit from a historical perspective. I quote him at length because of the thorough way in which he has framed the topic:

> The second grand shift, modernity to postmodernity (the first being premodernity to modernity), is pictured as a transition from an anthrocentric world to either a centerless or a polycentric world characterized by the loss of the subject. According to the purveyors of postmodernity, the moderns used the myths of Reason, the "universal man," and progress to promote universality. The result was that the human world became a unidimensional world, with modern historians employing their master narratives for Eurocentric purposes. History was the arena of Europeans and a few others; Africa was bereft of history—politics and philosophy— was occupied by males; females lived in the ahistorical world of the private sphere. For the emerging postmodern historians of the late-twentieth century, the polycentric shift has produced a turn in which all human lived experience became the subject matter of history. Everyone and everything had a history, even abstractions like tastes, anger, cleanliness, and sexuality. Multiplicity supplanted universality; multidimensionality replaced unidimensionality; multidirectional analysis marginalized progress as a linear approach. Reality, if reality existed, by definition stretched historical categories.[22]

Obviously, postmodernity has an agenda. Its agenda is to free human beings from the shackles of pure reason, unattainable objectivity, oppressive universalism, and a limited view on reality. Recognizing the limits and pitfalls of modernity, postmodern thinkers have emerged out of the darkness of modernity in order to more accurately understand the world in which they live.[23] Is their "corrective" enterprise one that African Americans want or need to join? Anderson thinks so.

> A second warrant for pressing beyond ontological blackness is that the idea is incommensurable with the demand for a new cultural politics of black identity that meaningfully relates to the conditions of postmodern North American life...The new cultural

---

[22]David D. Daniels, III, "'God's All in This Place': God and Historical Writing in the Postmodern Era," in *The Courage to Hope: From Black Suffering to Human Redemption,* ed. Quinton Hosford Dixie and Cornel West (Boston: Beacon Press, 1999), 5.

[23]Walter Lowe, *Theology and Difference: The Wound of Reason* (Bloomington, Ind.: Indiana University Press, 1993).

politics of difference takes seriously the ways that ontological blackness alienates African Americans who pursue genuine interests in personal fulfillment along class, gender, ethnic, and sexual differentials...those racial discourses that derive their legitimacy from ontological blackness are at odds with contemporary postmodern black life.[24]

Linking the agendas of postmodernity with the agenda of moving beyond ontological blackness seems to be problematic at best and disingenuous at worst. They do not appear to have the same agenda. Anderson and others are speaking from within the black community, where they feel oppressed by the cult of heroic genius and "demand" that they be supported in their quest for personal fulfillment along class, gender, ethnic, and sexual differentials. Their argument is that any cultural-political enterprise such as public theology that does not take their demand seriously has lost its legitimacy in representing the contemporary black community in its totality. The agenda that underlies this "personal demand" is fundamentally different from the agenda outlined earlier regarding postmodernity.

The cult of a new black cultural politics of difference seems driven by an individualism that is not found in the larger postmodern enterprise. Postmodernity seeks to widen the circle so that more voices and perspectives can be heard. In this sense the end is a more inclusive cultural world where no one is left out. Those who seek to move beyond ontological blackness also purport to advocate for more inclusion through the recognition of difference within the African American community. However, the emphasis on difference seems to be more interested in transcendent individualism than inclusion. That is, the transcendence that the cult of a new black cultural politics of difference seeks beyond racial apologetics, binary structures, and survival strategies also lies outside the group and has the limited goal of fulfilling individual, personal needs. Anderson links his perspectives with the work of Howard Thurman and Cornel West in order to defend against the assertion that his viewpoint ignores the real struggle blacks wage against racism or that he resists inclusion in the cultural life of African Americans.

Both Thurman and West exhibit aspects of the religious criticism that I advance. Both thinkers are African Americans who take their point of departure in the critique of culture from African American life in the United States. While consciously aware of the pervasive existential influences of white racism on black life, neither thinker regards racist influences as so pervasive as to render black life totalized by its demonic consequences.

---

[24]Anderson, *Beyond Ontological Blackness,* 15–16.

Both Thurman and West hold open the possibility that the apparently binary oppositions that characterize racial discourse can be transcended. But transcendence requires a cause that is sufficiently categorical to include within itself both the cultural aspects of group life and personality. For Thurman the dialectics of race is transcended in the idea of the beloved community. For West radical democracy serves the function of transcendence. I call the elements of transcendence that these thinkers commend *cultural fulfillment.*[25]

I would be more convinced that the cult of a new black cultural politics of difference is interested in a transcendence that appreciates personality *and* group life if there were anything presented that affirmed the cultural aspects of group life. Group life in the form of ontological blackness is presented as a demonic force that strangles the individual spirit and ignores difference. There are, however, significant ways in which group life contributes to the cultural fulfillment of individuals and celebrates difference. Group life or community supplies many of the basic human needs and subjective goods Anderson describes. Moreover, according to developmental theory the cultural fulfillment of the individual that Anderson seeks is a limited goal. The most highly developed individual personality is one that views itself as integrally interconnected with the selves of others.[26]

As a cultural critic perhaps Anderson does not feel that he has to address this question, but as a pastoral theologian I feel compelled to ask it for him: "In the final analysis, to what end does the kind of transcendence that he commends as cultural fulfillment lead?" What is the vision that the new cultural politics of difference has in mind? Anderson gives us glimpses when he states that the meeting of human needs and the provision of subjective goods will result in a cultural fulfillment that "individuals require for alleviating subjective alienation, assuring subjective equilibrium, and realizing positive personalities."[27] He concludes that the black community needs a new public theology that will "take seriously the ethnic, class, gender, and sexual differentials that structure contemporary African American public life,"[28] that will include revealing the grotesque features of African American life so as to accurately reflect the complexity of African American

---

[25]Ibid., 48–49.

[26]See Robert Kegan's *The Evolving Self* (Cambridge, Mass.: Harvard University Press, 1992), in which he describes five constitutions of the self that evolve over a lifetime. The fourth stage is the "institutional self" or individual self, but the final stage is the "inter-institutional self," a self that recognizes that its being relies on its interdependence with others. Also see Carolyn C. McCrary's discussion of Thurman and interdependence in "Interdependence as a Normative Value in Pastoral Counseling with African Americans," in *The Recovery of Black Presence: An Interdisciplinary Exploration,* ed. Randall C. Bailey and Jacquelyn Grant, (Nashville: Abingdon Press, 1995), 159–75.

[27]Anderson, *Beyond Ontological Blackness,* 49.

[28]Ibid., 157.

life and culture. The vision and goals that Anderson presents are somewhat vague and imprecise. As guiding principles they describe certain attributes and attitudes that should be present and applied in the construction of an African American future, but we do not have a clear indication of what that future would look like if these attributes and attitudes existed.

Constructing a Nonapologetic Black Cultural Genius Response

In the remainder of this chapter I would like to take up Anderson's invitation to develop a public theology that is not delegitimatized by ontological blackness, takes seriously the need for a realistic picture of black cultural life without reverting to the "grotesquery of postmodern blackness," and demonstrates appreciation for group life.

Such a pastoral theology lays claim to the adaptive genius of a people, but not a genius that is apologetic or compensatory. Instead, a pastoral theology that takes seriously the need to move beyond ontological blackness frames the adaptive genius of a people as both a response to external pressures and a unique and creative way of fashioning that response. Rightly understood, the response is a reaction to an external event, but it is also an interior enterprise of meaning making that results in the formation of a distinctive culture. For indeed, culture is composed of a number of elements. "The construction of culture is about the creation, accumulation, and passing on of a group's knowledge—the strategies, techniques, symbols, artifacts, and systems of meaning that foster survival."[29] The cultural product is unique and distinctive, not essential. That is, the wide variety of ways in which a people respond to a set of circumstances connotes the unique and distinctive dimension of the culture.

Yet the unique and distinctive cultural response is conditioned by a set of common experiences that a people encounter precisely because of their racial categorization by the larger context within which they live. The racial categorization by others cannot be denied, but that racial categorization need not define who a people are. Indeed, the response can be a response of resistance that creates an alternative identity, replete with a full and wide set of self-understandings and definitions. And in that expansive set of self-definitions a people appropriate a culture that allows them to thrive and flourish, as well as survive. It is not a question of either/or, but of both/ and. A black pastoral theology cannot help but be conditioned by the historical events of the black past. However, the distinctive rather than essential way that African Americans have shaped their response is unique and has been determined by them. And the defining element of the cultural

---

[29]Cheryl Townsend Gilkes, "'Some Folk Get Happy and Some Folk Don't: Diversity, Community, and African American Christian Spirituality,'" in *The Courage to Hope: From Black Suffering to Human Redemption,* ed. Quinton Hosford Dixie and Cornel West, (Boston: Beacon Press, 1999), 206.

response is not an essential element, but the totality of the different individual responses within the larger black cultural response.

Nor should a black pastoral theology valorize a people or deny the "grotesque" within and among them. To do so would be to deny the opportunity for the full expression of a unique and distinctive black culture. I would employ another word for what the proponents of a new culture of political difference call "grotesque." Almost any other word or words would do, but I am drawn to *multiplicity of response.* Multiplicity of response recognizes both the differences that are housed in the notion of multiplicity and the cohesiveness of these different responses that are distinctive.

A historical review of the life of African Americans reveals a vast number of creative responses and contributions to the American experience. The responses range from a complete rejection of America as a home and return to Africa to the adoption of America as the new home of African Americans with a commitment to move America closer to its stated ideals. In between these poles is reflected the reality, limits, challenges, and lessons that African Americans have encountered on the way toward full humanity in America. The totality of these multiple responses constitutes African American culture. It is a culture that is multidetermined, multidimensional, multifaceted, and irreducible to a singular essence. However, it is circumscribed by a structure of commitment to achieve full humanity for African Americans. And here Malcolm X's (and before him Martin Delany's) inducement to strive for freedom "by any means necessary" takes on new meaning. The pronouncement is not exclusively a militant call to arms but is an encouragement to exercise the full variety of options available in the struggle for freedom.

Every person is, in certain respects,

a. like all other persons,

b. like some other persons

c. like no other person[30]

When Kluckhohn and Murray state that some persons are alike in certain respects, they are referring to cultural identity. A culture by definition is a body of perspectives, rituals, experiences, and so on, shared by a group of persons. The identity of individual persons within that cultural group is significantly influenced by that culture. Thus, they have a cultural identity that is integral to their individual identity and vice versa. As cultures shape the persons within them, there is somewhat of a coercive dimension to that shaping. Cultures determine what contributes positively or negatively to the culture, what lies within and without the culture. Without these

---

[30]Clyde Kluckhohn and Henry A. Murray, "Personality Formation: The Determinants," in *Personality in Nature, Society, and Culture,* ed. Clyde Kluckhohn and Henry A. Murray, (New York: Alfred A. Knopf, 1953), 53.

evaluative elements within a culture, the culture as a whole risks promoting life-robbing rather than life-giving forces within its midst.

At times, though, there will be friction within the culture about what it designates as life-robbing and life-giving. The play *Fiddler on the Roof* is an excellent example of that conflict. Each of Tevye's daughters challenges her culture's tradition as she pursues her individual dream of fulfillment. The cult of the new black cultural politics of difference wants to defend and preserve the right of individual blacks to seek their individual fulfillment without the criticism and coercive force of ontological blackness. This is a dilemma for the African American community. On the one hand, the community seeks to "impose" its culture as a means of providing individuals with a cultural identity and the cultural stuff necessary to ward off racial categorization. On the other, individual persons within the culture may experience the imposition of cultural identity formation as stifling their individual personal identity, thereby obstructing their fulfillment.

I believe that there is a solution to this dilemma. Ideally a culture provides its members with a cultural identity that contributes to their sense of belonging to a group that shares a common history and set of experiences but also allows persons to express their own individual sense of what it means to be a member of that culture. The question is, How can a culture ensure the integrity of its traditions while at the same time support individuals within it to determine their individual (different) expressions of that culture? Here is where womanist ethicists make a valuable contribution to the work of African Americans to secure a connected and fulfilled future.

Womanist Ethics Points the Way

With a devotion to the maintenance of good relationships, womanist ethicists move the issue of the ontological away from the cultural feature of blackness to the ethical arena of what contributes to the health, well-being, and survival of black people. The issue no longer is what fundamentally is blackness (what is essential blackness), but what fundamentally empowers black people to achieve full humanity.

Emilie Townes best exemplifies this new direction in womanist ethics as she focuses on the death-dealing policies and practices affecting the health of African Americans.[31] Her most recent work examines the ways that African Americans in the past (Tuskegee syphilis experiment) and in the present (toxic waste dumps in black communities) are easy prey for those in power to utilize for high-risk enterprises.[32] Townes sounds the alarm about these practices and rallies blacks to collectively resist projects that

---

[31]Emilie M. Townes, *Breaking the Fine Rain of Death: African American Health Issues and a Womanist Ethic of Care* (New York: Continuum, 1998), 81–106.
[32]Emilie M. Townes, *In a Blaze of Glory: Womanist Spirituality as Social Witness* (Nashville: Abingdon Press, 1995), 55.

put blacks at risk. Townes recognizes that in these situations the collective resistance of African Americans supersedes any strategy of individual personal fulfillment. In these situations neither the identification of essential blackness nor the affirmation of difference alone will successfully combat the threat to African American health. However, as people together recognize the threat to their communities and mobilize their individual efforts into a collective resistance, then the cult of black heroic genius, coupled with the cult of the new black cultural politics of difference, move toward the survival and fulfillment of black humanity.

What would a black pastoral theology look like that took seriously the postmodern critique of ontological blackness but did not reject completely black essentialism? Such a black pastoral theology would be driven by the dynamic of a composite both/and rather than an exclusionary dynamic of either/or. The commitment to a both/and dynamic would necessarily include a commitment to hold disparate and often-conflicting manifestations of a culture in tension with one another. No aspect of the cultural reality of a people would be ignored. Rather, every effort would be made to pay attention to the contribution the multiplicity of responses makes to the collective song sung by a whole people.

The black pastoral theology of such a people would recognize that their genius functions not just to engage in compensatory apologetics that extol genius and deny difference, but that the genius of this creative people has fashioned a variety of ways to survive and strive for freedom in the face of threats to their existence. In this black pastoral theology, black culture would be understood as both a multiplicity of responses to white racism and the means and sign of transcendence of that racism. In this light the multiplicity of response is not a counterbalance but a reflection of the reality, limits, challenges, and lessons learned from the past that together give shape and form to contemporary African American culture.

A black pastoral theology for today recognizes that a collective identity has been the transmitter of African American culture that has enabled a people to survive but also that it should allow for different expressions of African American culture that constitute the richness of that collective cultural identity. In order to avoid a chaotic and meaningless wandering of individuals whose limited goal is the freedom to be different or a closed collective mind-set whose group think rejects alternative life-giving perspectives, a vision for the future coupled with ethical guidelines needs to be incorporated into a black pastoral theology.

This does not mean that the vision is a singular, static one to which all must pledge allegiance. However, there has to be some goal or direction or trajectory identified, or else a people will wander in the wilderness. Within the larger goal, direction, or trajectory, different strategies, steps, and perspectives should exist. The multiplicity of perspectives helps guarantee a well-conceived and thought-out vision. Yet some goals, directions, and perspectives are more life-giving and destiny-fulfilling than others. Critical ethical reflection on the visions needs to be a part of a comprehensive black pastoral theology. I conjure the Joshua story again as an aid in this constructive project.

Black Cultural Identity and the Conjure of Joshua

If there ever was a story in the Bible that demonstrated the worst of the heroic genius image, it is the story of Joshua. Joshua is hero writ large. He is God's hand-picked successor to Moses; he is obedient, strong, and courageous; he makes no mistakes; his extraordinary wisdom, fairness, and capacity to inspire a people help to guarantee their survival; and there is nothing "grotesque" about him.

Although it is not a racial apologetic, the book of Joshua is somewhat of an apologetic in that it was written as a response to the then-recent captivity of the ancient Israelites at the hands of the Babylonians. An enslaved, dispersed, and demoralized people needed a story that would glorify their past, present them as conquering warriors, and renew a sense of pride and hope within them. The exaggerations that are often found in racial apologetics and cults of heroic genius are also found in the story of Joshua. Nothing in Joshua is ever done on a small scale. A whole people participate in the rituals; the towns they invade are destroyed totally, and nothing is left to remain. The drama and spectacle of Joshua is worthy of a Cecil B. DeMille motion picture. The story's binary structure is rigidly in place. It is the ancient Israelites versus the Canaanites, those who support the campaign (even Rahab, who is not an Israelite) versus those who do not support the campaign (including Achan, who is an Israelite), sparing life versus destruction of all that lives. From the cultural fulfillment perspective, Joshua seems to have little to offer in moving beyond ontological blackness. Again, Joshua seems to be a problematic conjure for contemporary African Americans when viewed from a postmodern perspective.

Adaptive Genius

Yet if we apply the "grotesquery" of postmodern blackness to the story of Joshua, there is much that Joshua does offer to contemporary African American life and culture. Joshua tells the story of the adaptive genius of a people. Not unlike the ancient Israelites, blacks in America have exhibited the adaptive creativity necessary to survive and strive for freedom in the face of real threats to their existence. The grotesque or multiplicity of responses found in the creative genius of black people is a reflection of the full panoply of adaptations that blacks have made to the reality of white racism. This multiplicity of responses across the decades represent the challenges faced, the lessons learned, and the genius accumulated in African American culture.

In Joshua we encounter the obedience and disobedience, the mercy and the mercilessness, the "racial" essence and the "racial" pluralism of the ancient Israelites. They possess a collective identity that has been for them the transmitter of culture. They have brought aspects of this culture with them and have found the struggle in Canaan an inducement to remember and renew the essential elements of that culture. Yet no matter how essential and necessary the collective cultural witness has been, the conquering Israelites were open to difference. Within their midst they allowed for individuals and individual tribes to exercise their different contributions to the struggle to claim their inheritance.

The Ethical Dimension

More than anything, the story of Joshua points to the need for African Americans to pay attention to the ethical dimensions of the struggle to survive and transcend. As was indicated earlier, the critical evaluative element in the postmodern freedom movement is not essentialism but ethical human determinism. That is, instead of examining each aspect of African American cultural expression and asking whether it reflects that which is essential about black life and culture, the question to be asked is does this aspect of African American culture contribute to the destiny God has determined for African Americans: full humanity? This critical ethical question needs to be applied to the variety of different proposals for black freedom. When this question is asked, it will take the form of a number of subquestions, including the following:

• Is the legacy of the black tradition being honored?
• In what ways will the survival of black people be preserved?
• How will the fulfillment of black people be enhanced?
• Is there a place for difference?
• How are black community needs and resources addressed?

These are the questions that should be applied to every enterprise that seeks to promote black survival and transcendence.

Cultural Essentialism

In the story of Joshua the genius of ancient Israel enters into the promised land. It was the essentialism of that culture that sustained them in the wilderness and brought them to the shores of the Jordan. But would that which had been essential in the past be life-giving and destiny-fulfilling in this new time and place? Apparently so. Former rituals, faithfully practiced, guaranteed bread for survival and a renewed identity through circumcision for generations in the future. Rituals of setting up markers and stones played the triple role of employing former practices to mark a present event that would remind those in the future what had happened

(Gilgal and Shechem). But even as these practices were carried out, ethical questions were brought to bear. Was the legacy of the Israelite tradition regularly and rightfully honored in the Passover and circumcision rituals? The answer to this question is decidedly yes. In fact, the circumcision at Gilgal reinstituted a tradition in the Israelite faith that had been absent for forty years of wandering in the wilderness. A new generation was incorporated into the covenant. In keeping the Passover, the Israelites kept faith with their tradition and were blessed with increased self-sufficiency as a result. Marking the places where significant events took place and participating in rites of purification helped maintain the traditions as well.

The ritual of Passover anticipated the ancient Israelites' ability to grow food for themselves and thereby enhanced their prospects for physical survival. The circumcision ritual reconstituted their cultural identity and thereby enhanced the prospects for the survival of their cultural identity. The altar built by the Transjordan tribes as a sign of remembrance fostered the survival of a connection between the Canaanite Israelites and the Transjordan Israelites. More important than the battles themselves, the faithful adherence to the traditions secured the survival of the ancient Israelites physically, culturally, and relationally.

What ethical principles are present in Joshua regarding the provision for difference? Opportunities for individual cultural expression, along with openness to the presence of different groups and personalities, mark Joshua. Rahab and the Gibeonites represent an alternative presence within the Israelite people. The Transjordan tribes are permitted to settle on the other side of the Jordan in a different location from the larger group. The story of Joshua includes the "grotesquery" of Achan, whose disregard for herem jeopardizes the Israelites' campaign. The death of Achan and his family points to an ethical principle regarding the relative merits of individual and corporate fulfillment. Fulfillment of the individual at the expense or harm of the corporate is morally wrong. The book of Joshua does not deny difference but does hold that the expression of individual cultural fulfillment must not harm the group. Individual cultural expression does have its limits. At the point that individual cultural fulfillment jeopardizes the survival and fulfillment of others, its ethical and moral privilege is forfeited.

The best example of this point in the black community today involves rap music. Many in the African American community would certainly signify (and signify against) rap music as different. Yet as Michael Eric Dyson has eloquently opined, rap music is a vibrant response of young blacks to the hopelessness, despair, and harm they see resident in the black community.[33] Rap music represents African American heroic response, as well as the grotesquery of black postmodernity. As one of the multitude of

---

[33]Michael Eric Dyson, *Between God and Gangsta Rap: Bearing Witness to Black Culture* (New York: Oxford University Press, 1996), 161–86.

cultural expressions, how should rap music's contribution to the freedom and liberation of African Americans be evaluated? Rap music certainly honors the creative spirit found in the African American musical tradition that has spawned the spirituals, the blues, jazz, gospels, rock and roll, and hip-hop. The force, drive, and energy of rap expresses the deep and pained response of a generation to the contemporary scene and their prospects (more accurately, lack of prospects) for abundant life within it. Like musical expressions before it, rap seeks its own creative way of making a statement in the present moment about what it means to be black in America. The legacy of a people struggling to survive and transcend the harsh realities of oppression is reflected in rap music.

From an empowerment ethic, however, some of the music of rap and the culture of rap may not preserve the survival and fulfillment of blacks. Also, rap music seems to respond to certain needs and resources in the black community but may also deplete some resources necessary for meeting the needs within the African American community. In an ironic twist, rap music's initial intent to produce a music that would garner a respect of its own has resulted in an intracultural war fueled by mutual accusations of disrespect. Music that once was an expression of the self has now become an extension of the self. Any critique of a rap artist's music has become a critique of the person him- or herself. Consequently, the response to such critique may come in the form of a counter-rap, or it may come in the form of violent, physical attack.

Not all rap artists "compete" with one another in life-threatening ways. However, some behavior among rap artists does jeopardize the survival of blacks, not only through the actual taking of life but also through the models presented of how to handle disputes. Again, in another ironic twist, rap music began as a unique and distinct musical style that sought to be different from its predecessors or contemporary musical expressions. Yet the cultural critiques of one another demonstrate little tolerance for difference among them.

Perhaps the strongest criticism leveled against some rap music is the denigration of women in the lyrics. Black women will not find fulfillment in those lyrics. Rather, they will find put-down, name-calling, and dehumanization. Is any expression for the sake of the new cultural politics of difference to be embraced by African Americans? I think not. I certainly want to support the freedom of all within the African American community to give self-expression to the ways in which they want to make a cultural contribution. However, when the expression of difference demeans and fails to contribute to full humanity, the benefit of that kind of difference requires examination. The mistake that the cult of the new black cultural politics of difference makes is saying that difference means fulfillment. Difference does not automatically mean fulfillment. A discernment process must be put in place in order to determine from an ethical stance whether or not particular cultural expressions within the African American community do, in fact, lead to fulfillment (or wholeness, or full humanity). Without such ethical discernment the multitude of cultural responses can lead to a cacophony of tragic proportions.

The Role of the Black Church

In light of the identity formation challenges facing the black community, the black church has a unique and distinctive role to play in addressing the crisis of black identity through processes of moral and ethical discernment. Womanist theologians have begun the task of applying such critical ethical discernment to the life of black people, particularly in the area of class separation among blacks.[34] The other contribution that womanist ethicists make in addition to a model for blending essential blackness with cultural difference is how to refashion evaluations of the effectiveness of the various cultural agendas in the advancement of black people. Ontological blackness identifies rootedness in essential blackness as a primary ingredient in the black struggle for liberation. The new black cultural politics of difference identifies the freedom for individual expression of the self as the primary ingredient in postmodern blackness.

Womanist ethicists urge African Americans to ask these questions: Can we be a people of faith in the midst of diversity? That is, can the black church enter into partnership with a variety of persons with different backgrounds and gifts so as to mobilize the most effective force against oppression? What are we teaching the people? That is, are we teaching them how to be family and community in those ways that have sustained and protected a people in the past? What are we doing for the spiritual health of the people? That is, are we worshiping and living together in such a way as to portray life-giving images of blackness, maleness, femaleness, age, income, and sexuality as well and countering any voice that tells black people they are less than? What are we saying to the people? That is, are we reinforcing among ourselves that we are worthy of love and respect that must be continually claimed as well as fought for in order to retain? A Joshua church is one in which these questions are asked repeatedly *and* the answers to those questions are lived out in the ministries of the church.[35]

The Joshua church is a home over Jordan where black people in all of their diversity live out their life of faith together. The Joshua church is a place of safety and affirmation where persons are assisted in forming their unique identity and contributing to the church's mission in God to bring

---

[34]Townes, *In a Blaze of Glory*, 120–44; Marcia Y. Riggs, *Awake, Arise, and Act: A Womanist Call for Black Liberation* (Cleveland: Pilgrim Press, 1994); Cheryl Sanders, *Empowerment Ethics for a Liberated People: A Path to African American Social Transformation* (Minneapolis: Fortress Press, 1995).

[35]Townes, *In a Blaze of Glory*, 140–44.

all to full humanity. In that formation process of individual and collective identity no one is excluded. The ethical imperative that drives the Joshua church is that the survival and fulfillment of a people depends on their commitment to the inclusion of all, as well as their commitment to resist individual and personal fulfillment at the expense of the group. The Joshua church is a both/and church that believes that the cultural fulfillment needs of the individual can be met in the group life of the church. The survival and fulfillment agendas of the church are not antithetical to each other, but make up two complementary thrusts of the church's mission that *together* guarantee both survival and fulfillment.

Each local black church must find its own particular way of being a Joshua church, leading its people through individual and collective identity formation to a home over Jordan guaranteeing survival and fulfillment. In this chapter I have suggested some ways of thinking about cultural identity formation that might be helpful to churches in that enterprise. Before closing this chapter, I would like to offer three vignettes of ministry that I think reflect the ideas and images discussed earlier.

The first vignette returns to Rev. Jeremiah Wright and his Pizza with the Pastor session with teens in his church. Throughout the Bible special attention is given to the needs of those who are most vulnerable to the exigencies of life: widows, children, the disabled, the sick, the poor, and the oppressed. In the African American community today those who are most vulnerable are our children. African American families where there is a single parent with children are the poorest families of any ethnic group. Candy and pop companies target black children and contribute to the higher risk of obesity that exists in the African American community.[36] Father absence in the African American community has left many of our children without the benefits of an intact family. The suicide and homicide rates among black males are disproportionately high, and too many of our teenage girls are giving birth and having to raise children too early and with too little support. Many of our teenagers live a wilderness existence and are in desperate need of guidance over Jordan to a place of safety and fulfillment, a home.

Pizza with the Pastor is an occasion where teenagers can obtain answers to their important questions, get information and share insights with one another, receive guidance and give feedback, be affirmed and support one another, and receive a blessing and give a blessing. In the course of these conversations the teenagers have the opportunity to clarify their identities, learn who they are, and explore what they believe, why they see things the

---

[36]In a presentation at the Pediatric Academic Societies Annual Meeting on April 28, 2001, Dr. Anjali Jain and Manasi Tirodkar reported that commercials featured during black prime time televisions shows (e.g., *The Parkers* and *The Jamie Foxx Show*) are more likely to promote candy and soda than commercials aired during general prime time shows (e.g., *Friends* and *Frasier*).

way they do, and where they are headed. Pastor Wright, as representative of the collective body, is making sure that this remnant of the people on the journey are not lost. In these conversations they come to know themselves as individuals but also come to know themselves as part of a larger community and enterprise that has the power and potential to deliver them from the evil that endangers them. In these conversations Pastor Wright continually asks the teens to make connections between African American heritage and the challenges they face daily in their lives. Not all of black heritage is heroic genius, yet all of it speaks to some challenge confronting black people today. Pastor Wright challenges them to make the connections, and in so doing he assists them in bringing forward a rich cultural heritage for identity formation in the present and future.

The second vignette is of a pastor in Montgomery, Alabama, who raps with the teenagers in his church.[37] Rap itself is not viewed as demonic by Rev. Joseph Rembert of the St. Paul AME Church. He recognizes that rap is the language art that teenagers are employing to express their sense of who they are and what they are about. Moreover, Rev. Rembert sees rap as a vehicle through which he can begin to address the issues black teenagers are facing–drugs, violence, peer pressure, and so on–and do so in a positive manner. In his rap he tries to directly link the challenges teens are encountering with a Christian life perspective. Thus, rap takes on a positive slant as it tries to get youth excited about their spiritual relationship with Jesus through rap. Here are a few examples of his raps:

> While I guess you all are wondering just why I'm here
> Because no other preacher would dare appear
> When we do this all the critics will tease us
> But I don't care, I came to talk about Jesus

> Now I like Michael Jackson; he's a real big thrill
> But he didn't die on Calvary's hill
> It was my man Jesus who gave his life
> To save my children, me and my wife

Rev. Rembert sometimes takes on the voice of struggling teens in his raps:

> Now I used to be jive, and I smoked my dope
> Trying to stay high so that I could cope
> But my troubles didn't leave they just stayed around
> And they seemed a little worse when I came down
> Some of my friends they turned to crime
> Many of them are still doing their time

---

[37]Jannell McGrew from *The Montgomery Adviser,* in *The United Methodist Reporter,* 21 July 2000.

But I was lucky, and I stayed out of jail
But could feel my soul getting closer to hell
Then I heard about Jesus, the father's son
Who battled death and the grave, and I heard he won.
Man, oh man, what a victory!
He opened my eyes and made me see

Cognizant of the need that black youth have for spiritual resources to battle the forces that block survival and liberation, Rev. Rembert utilizes a form of cultural expression that black youth have embraced to make the message easily accessible and attractive.

The third vignette involves a couple who were referred to me for counseling by their pastor. Sandra and James are both thirty-five. Sandra is a bank teller, and James is an insurance salesman. They have been married for ten years and have no children. Their disagreement about having children was one of the reasons why they sought the help of their pastor, who referred them to me. Sandra was interested in having children; James was reluctant. For James bringing a child into their marriage was a risky venture. On the one hand, Sandra had suffered from panic attacks in the past, and he was concerned about her ability to cope with a newborn. James also saw how involved Sandra was with her family of origin. Sandra grew up in a family where there was much emotional abuse and neglect. James experienced Sandra as constantly intervening with her family to stop a fight and/or provide money as she tried to create a sense of peace in that household. He worried about how Sandra would handle simultaneously the commitment to her family of origin and to a child. He feared that Sandra would feel too guilty either about shortchanging her family of origin or shortchanging their child. Sandra brought to counseling a concern about James's decreased interest in sex.

During the course of the counseling we addressed the concerns and difficulties that Sandra and James initially brought to the counseling. James was able to be more physically affectionate with Sandra, and Sandra exercised better limits on her involvement with her family. On the issue of children Sandra and James decided that there were many ways they could agree on to nurture children. Sandra reflected in counseling on her childhood wish that someone would provide better nurture and guidance to her. Sandra could see that like herself as a child, the girls in her neighborhood could benefit from an opportunity to get together with adults who would provide some guidance and direction.

Consequently, Sandra approached the parents of girls between the ages of eight and fourteen who lived in her neighborhood and attended her church to see if they would be interested in their daughters' becoming Girl Scouts. After getting a positive response from a number of parents, Sandra decided to establish a scout troop at her church. Sandra's passion for this project was intense, and it was important to her that James be supportive of it. She wanted James to not only endorse the idea but also to help in the recruitment of children, the preparation of publicity, and the coordination of scheduled activities. For Sandra it was important to be seen by James as a capable and competent person. In addition to her dissatisfaction with James's lack of physical affection and his impression of her as fragile, Sandra resented the dynamics in the marriage that had James in an overfunctioning position that blocked all her efforts at fulfillment. If having a child was not a viable way of deconstructing the "less than" status she felt in the marriage, then constructing a resource to meet the needs of the girls around her was the method she would employ.

Through her initiative and desire Sandra was able to begin a project that would promote her fulfillment in a way other than having her own child. Moreover, James would be a partner with her in this enterprise. And he would not be calling the shots. Instead, through his support he would be indicating that he trusted Sandra's leadership in this project and that he was willing to give his endorsement through his participation.

From an individualistic cultural fulfillment perspective the prospects for a resolution of the problems between Sandra and James were limited. Either they split in order to fulfill their own needs, or one of them had to capitulate to the other in order to preserve a homeostatic balance. When a collective identity perspective is joined with a cultural fulfillment perspective, other options emerge. The resolution to Sandra's and James's problems were no longer set in a binary structure such that the solution was either "my way or the highway." Rather, they were able to discern a solution in which both sets of needs and desires were met. Neither may have been met perfectly, but enough of their individual needs were met in their shared solution that they both felt sufficiently fulfilled.

More important, their commitment to the survival and fulfillment of the girls in their community provided an essential resource for the resolution of their personal conflict. Group life was not a deterrent to individual fulfillment but a necessary factor in its realization. The church's role in this outcome was vital in that the church as a community resource made the initial referral. Behind the church's referral was a sense that the enhancement of both Sandra's and James's lives lay in their ability to find a way of satisfying individual, personal needs, as well as in fulfilling the commitment each of them had made to their marriage. The church as a partner with other community resources coordinated with the resource of a pastoral counselor in order to address the dual sets of commitments that it viewed Sandra and James struggling with. As Sandra and James found ways of living out the dual sets of commitments, they turned to the church as both a resource and arena for addressing their own and their community's cultural fulfillment.

Sandra's project of guiding African American girls in her neighborhood certainly had ontological blackness dimensions. The project was a response to the racism in America that threatens the survival and fulfillment of young black girls. The group activity of the girls was geared toward the heroic genius of the African American past, as well as toward fostering reliance on the group as a definer of identity and a resource for basic human needs.

As for the marriage and my counseling approach, I was committed to Sandra and James as individuals and as an individual couple but also felt a commitment to the African American community to help create marital relationships whose intactness contributes to the survival and well-being of the community.

Conversely, I also felt that the fulfillment of Sandra and James as individuals and as a couple would be better secured through their participation in the survival of their community. Certainly the danger existed that if Sandra involved herself in the uplift work with the girls in her neighborhood, she would risk stressing herself out even more. But Sandra needed to learn another way of being in community that was different from emotional abuse, overextension, and stress. In this work Sandra could learn how to better negotiate competing demands on her person, gain support from others around her, and meet her need to care for children.

There was also danger for James in his participation in the work of guiding girls in the neighborhood. In his marriage to Sandra, James was beginning to conclude that problems with members of one's extended family meant only trouble and that the best response was to stay away. James needed to learn that becoming involved in the lives of persons who were struggling to survive need not mean endless frustration and wasted resources. In fact, the resentment he received from Sandra for advising on the sidelines was eradicated. His active participation made his advice and counsel more acceptable.

The drama of Sandra's and James's marriage is set in the larger context of their local church's cultural identity journey as a Joshua church. St. Andrew's Methodist celebrated its fiftieth anniversary five years ago. Recently the church has been going through a number of different transitions. First, the neighborhood has been changing from white to black since 1975. In 1965 the neighborhood was 75 percent white and 25 percent black. By 1995 the neighborhood was 95 percent black and 5 percent white. In 1965 the church was 90 percent white and 10 percent black. By 1995 the church was 99 percent black and 1 percent white. A new pastor was appointed by the bishop in 1995. Prior to that appointment all the pastors of St. Andrew's had been white. Pastor Strong was the first black pastor appointed at St. Andrew's. Over the last twenty-five years the church had been losing membership, and the church building was in serious disrepair.

Under Pastor Strong's leadership the church has made a conscious effort to meet the categorical and subjective needs of the congregation through the adoption of an ontological blackness approach. Using black theology's encouragement to establish God's realm through the liberation of black people, Rev. Strong sought to empower his church and community by drawing upon the heritage of the black tradition. Spirituals and gospel music were added to standard anthems in worship. Vestments and altar cloths with African designs appeared in the sanctuary. Rev. Strong's preaching accentuated the need for the members of the congregation to struggle together to affirm themselves and strengthen their community.

It was out of this context that Sandra's plan to develop a Girl Scout program surfaced. In part Sandra was responding to a challenge from her pastor, which in turn was a response to the call from God to claim the place that had been given to the people of St. Andrew's. There are a vitality and essential life force in the cult of heroic genius that energize a people for combating racism and its demonic forces. Appropriating aspects of heroic genius shapes the individual and collective identity of a people so that they stand strong in the battle to preserve their sense of destiny and promised fulfillment. Whatever corrective the cult of the new black cultural politics of difference brings to ontological blackness, there must be a recognition that the cult of heroic genius does provide resources for identity formation that are essential for cultural fulfillment.

In a postmodern age, the most effective postmodern black pastoral theology incorporates both ontological blackness and the new black cultural politics of difference for the sake of identify formation required for successful claim of a home over Jordan.

CHAPTER 4

Connecting a Disconnected People

African Americans at the turn of the twenty-first century are living as disconnected as they have ever been since slavery, perhaps even more so. This disconnection can be found in a number of different areas. In this chapter we will focus on two areas of disconnection: (1) gender relationships and (2) class separation. Disconnection refers to the inability to come together for mutual support in a common enterprise. Whether that enterprise is intact families, viable neighborhoods, or cooperative projects for cultural and political empowerment, African Americans experience difficulty these days in finding ways to live and work together. Such living and working together become important if, as was suggested in the Introduction, there needs to be a collective enterprise carried out by African Americans in order for African Americans to survive.

This connecting has become especially difficult in a post–civil rights era. When integration and assimilation into America's mainstream did not materialize in the ways that Martin Luther King, Jr., Roy Wilkins, and Whitney Young envisioned, African Americans found themselves thrown back to an experience of wilderness wandering. Any number of attempts have been made to chart a course for the future, but the paths are often individualistic, both in their focus on personal achievement and in their resistance to cooperative effort. In the area of gender relationships, black women by the age of forty have given up on the prospect of marrying. The feeling seems to be that they can do just as well living a life and raising a child without the complications of marriage. Black men between the ages of twenty and forty-five, content to play the field unencumbered by family, are resisting getting married.

Black communities whose creation was the result of Jim Crow discrimination and racial cohesion formed networks of mutual support and dependency that enabled people to transcend the daily assaults on their person. In those neighborhoods blacks of every color, political persuasion, and economic and educational level lived together and made life viable. As opportunities opened for integration into those places that were at one time closed to blacks, a migration from the black ghetto ensued. However, the reception blacks received in these new locations was mixed, at best. Beverly Daniel Tatum writes about the "assimilation blues" blacks often contract when they integrate their lives with whites, and about the difficulties black children have had in developing an identity when there is no supportive structure for racial identity formation in the midst of an alienating environment.[1] Alienated from one another, black people struggle to survive and thrive. Many have become relational refugees, vulnerable to psychological and spiritual disease.[2]

In 1963 I responded to the call to go to Washington, D.C., and joined half a million people committed to the fight for justice and equality in the March on Washington. Thirty-three years later a similar call went out from Minister Louis Farrakhan for a million black men to converge on the nation's capital for repentance and recommitment to their families and communities. At moments like those the conflicting political and personal agendas of blacks seem able to be set aside. However, those moments seem few and far between in black history. Right now Clarence Thomas is unable to acknowledge the historical struggle that allows him to sit on the highest court in the land as he chips away at a body of legal decisions that supported his education and career development.[3] J. C. Watts refused to join the Congressional Black Caucus. With so few blacks in Congress, is not their voice diminished by his refusal to join with his black colleagues? Not only is the collective voice and thereby the power of black congresspeople lessened, the stage is set for the further dismantling of black people's power by those whose allegiance to political ideology supersedes a commitment to protect the most vulnerable in the society.[4]

---

[1]Beverly Daniel Tatum, *Assimilation Blues: Black Families in a White Community* (Northampton, Mass.: Hazel-Maxwell Publishing, 1992), and *"Why Are All the Black Kids Sitting Together in the Cafeteria?": And Other Conversations About Race* (New York: Basic Books, 1997).

[2]Edward Wimberly, *Relational Refugees* (Nashville: Abingdon Press, 2000).

[3]A. Leon Higginbotham, "An Open Letter to Justice Clarence Thomas from a Federal Judicial Colleague," in *Race-ing Justice, En-gendering Power: Essays on Anita Hill, Clarence Thomas, and the Construction of Social Reality,* ed. Toni Morrison (New York: Pantheon Books, 1992).

[4]Robert Singh, *The Congressional Black Caucus: Racial Politics in the U.S. Congress* (Thousand Oaks, Calif.: Sage Publications, 1998).

It is my contention that, along with an unclear cultural identity and lack of vision for the future, the disconnection among African Americans has contributed to the recent setbacks that have occurred for blacks in the socioeconomic indices of economics, politics, and health. The feminization of poverty in the African American community is a prime example. High divorce rates, low marriage rates, and high numbers of children born out of wedlock result in female-headed, single-parent households where the lack of two incomes, and in many instances even one, relegates that family to permanent poverty status.

At the base of this set of circumstances is the fact that black couples are not creating sustainable intact families. The disconnection between African American men and women impacts the economic viability of female-headed, single-parent families, which in turn jeopardizes the health of the women and children in those families. Without enough money for regular health care and nutritious diets, African American women and children are put at greater risk for illness and disease. Similarly, the separation between classes within the African American community hurts both those at the upper end of the socioeconomic structure and those at the lower end. When blacks who are financially better off leave the black neighborhood for the suburbs or wealthier communities, they create a void of leadership, financial resources, and commitment that contributes to the demise of that community's spirit. In communities where blacks who are financially better off locate, there often are not resources to foster racial pride, black cultural identity, and a sense of belonging. Affluent African Americans feel isolated, alienated, and "homeless." Consequently, as we have seen in the literature, issues of identity and belonging are becoming areas of great concern in the black community. This chapter seeks first to identify the factors associated with disconnection in the black community found in gender relations and class separation. Then the Joshua conjure will be employed to highlight some of the perspectives that can help restore a greater sense of connectedness.

The Disconnectedness between Black Men and Black Women

How bad is the disconnection between African American men and women? Pretty bad. In his recently completed, comprehensive research on the alienation between African American men and women, Orlando Patterson contends that "Afro-Americans are the most unpartnered and isolated group of people in America and quite possibly the world."[5] In order to substantiate this claim, Patterson draws on the 1996 General Social Survey conducted by the National Opinion Research Center at the University of Chicago. From this survey data Patterson is able to glean

---

[5]Orlando Patterson, *Rituals of Blood: Consequences of Slavery in Two American Centuries* (Washington, D.C.: Civitas/Counterpoint, 1998), 4.

empirical data on the nature of African American gender relations. For the sake of this discussion I will review Patterson's data in three sections: (1) attitudinal evaluations between the genders, (2) low marriage rates, and (3) high divorce rates.

When asked in the 1996 General Social Survey if they had felt "really angry" with someone in their family in the past months, African American women had the highest percent affirmative response (46.4 percent), compared with African American men (28.6 percent), European American women (38 percent), and European American men (18 percent). In addition 40 percent of African American women reported that they felt really angry longer (continuously or for several days) than European American women (33 percent) or men in either ethnic group (24 percent). Yet when asked how much they liked the person or people who made them angry, 44 percent of the African American women and 43 percent of the African American men responded that they liked the person or persons "a great deal." This compares to the responses of European American men and women, which were 20 percent and 36 percent respectively. Patterson concludes, "The facts are that Afro-Americans of both genders are getting angry with loved ones to a far greater degree than other people, and women are 62 percent more likely to be the ones feeling the pain."[6]

How likely is it that black men and women can easily resolve their conflicts? The data are not reassuring. When asked how responsible was the person they were angry at for the problem causing their anger, 64 percent of African American men and women identified the other person as fully responsible. Only 43 percent of European American men and 47 percent of European American women claimed the other person as fully responsible. When the question was turned around, and those surveyed were asked how responsible they were for the problem generating anger, 66 percent of African American women answered that they were in no way responsible, whereas 46 percent of African American men identified themselves as responsible. Patterson concludes, and I agree, "There is little hope for compromise here."[7] Given these figures, it is clear that there is a general underlying tension between black men and black women. Beyond these initial indications of disconnectedness are more specific factors for gender conflict that appear in the information associated with marriage rates and divorce rates.

Figure 1[8] shows how unpartnered African Americans are. The majority of African American men (64.4 percent) and women (72 percent) are unpartnered. Of those who have never been married, the percentage of African American men and women is nearly double that of European

---

[6]Ibid., 6.

[7]Ibid., 7.

[8]Figures 1–4 are from Patterson, *Rituals of Blood,* 57–60.

American men and women. **Figure 2**, which reports the number of Americans married, by ethnicity, gender, and age group, provides even more discouraging news. During the critical years of twenty-five to forty-five the majority of Americans are married, but for African American men

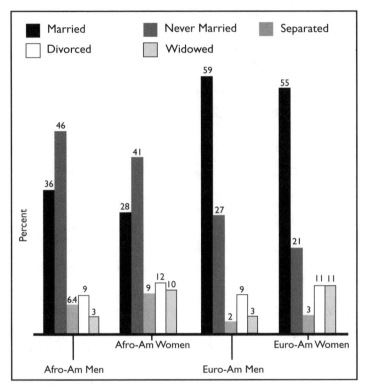

FIGURE 1: Marital Status of Persons over 15 by Gender and Ethnicity, March 1997

and women only 36 percent are married. Looking at gender differences over the life span we notice that the majority of African American men are married throughout the latter stages of the life cycle. However, for African American women, after their mid-forties the number who are married declines at a rate faster than any other group. Some of this decline can be explained by the death of spouses and divorce, but if we look at the percentage of unmarried women at age forty to forty-four by birth cohort and ethnicity (**Figure 3**), we see that there has been a marked increase for African American women born in the 1960s and after.

The final statistic to consider regarding marriage rates among African Americans is the number of years between marriage dissolution and remarriage. For both European American and African American women remarriage rates after a first marriage have been declining over the years.

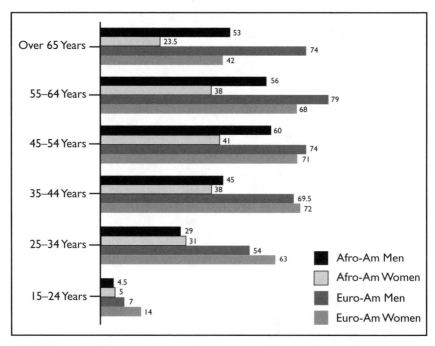

FIGURE 2: Percentage of Americans Married, by Age Group, Ethnicity, and Gender, 1996

However, for African American women the rate of decline has been sharper (fewer remarriages and longer intervals between marriages). The picture that emerges is that African American men and women have lower marriage rates, are getting married later in the life cycle, are twice as likely to remain unmarried, and, especially for African American women, are increasingly disinclined to remarry after dissolution of a first marriage.

How do we explain the disinclination to marry in the African American community? Three reasons for the low marriage rates have been most frequently cited: (1) the male marriage pool argument, (2) the female independence argument, and (3) the school enrollment argument.

The male marriage pool argument has been put forth by William Julius Wilson.[9] He argues that marriage rates have declined since the 1970s because the prospects for jobs for inner city young black men began to deteriorate. At a time in their lives when they would ordinarily be establishing a marital relationship on the way toward creating a family, they did not have the financial wherewithal to follow through on that desire.

---

[9]William Julius Wilson, *The Truly Disadvantaged: The Inner City, the Underclass, and Public Policy* (Chicago: The University of Chicago Press, 1987), and *When Work Disappears: The World of the New Urban Poor* (New York: Knopf, 1996).

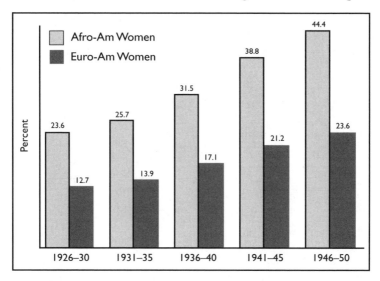

FIGURE 3: Percentage of Unmarried Women at Age 40–44, by Birth Cohort and Ethnicity

In addition, the high rates of incarceration and homicide have depleted the pool of African American men eligible for marriage. The female independence argument states that African American women have been a part of the larger movement among American women in which their economic independence has made them less dependent on marriage in order to secure their livelihood. Increased participation in the labor force, increased real income, the desire to pursue a career and delay marriage, and an increased sense of well-being apart from marriage have all contributed to women's—in this case, African American women's—decreased need to be married. The school enrollment thesis argues that younger African American women have increased their enrollment in school, which has delayed their entrance into the workforce and thereby delayed their marrying. Previously without these educational opportunities these women may have been more inclined to marry and marry earlier.

Patterson questions these explanations and for the male pool explanation makes the following observation regarding African American men and income: while the prospects for marrying increase as income increases, the line is not linear, but curvilinear. That is, African American men at the two extremes of the income curve mirror each other in terms of marriage rates. In fact, among all Americans, African American men in poverty are seven times more likely to marry. Patterson does not provide statistical data for the other two theses. He argues, though, that African American men's desirability for African American women with means cancels the female independence thesis as a contributor to low African American marriage rates. He also reports that the chief researchers[10] who put forth the school enrollment thesis were not able to produce data to support their own hypothesis.

If these three reasons do not explain the low marriage rates, then what does? Patterson convincingly argues that a complex set of factors interact to contribute to marriage rate decline and marital disruption increase in the African American community. These factors include the opportunity structure of marriage, or the varying degrees of readiness for marriage between black men and women depending on age, class, sexual experience, and demography; expected benefits from marriage; premarital behavior, including the presence of an out-of-wedlock child; family structure of the family of origin; religiosity; attitudes about infidelity; differing attitudes about gender roles and responsibilities; and sexual attitudes and practices. I will not go into the kind of detailed statistical analysis of these factors that Patterson does. However, I will provide one or two features of a few of these factors that are important to this discussion of connectedness among African Americans.

Benefits of Marriage

African American men and women have differing attitudes about the benefits of marriage and differing timetables regarding the fulfillment of those benefits. Shirley Hatchett has found that African American men place a greater emphasis on the expected emotional and expressive rewards of marriage, whereas African American women place greater emphasis on the instrumental and security aspects of marriage.[11] This conflict in expectations is further complicated by the factor of age. According to Scott J. South, African American unmarried men at all age levels have lower expectations of marriage than African American women do.[12] Not until they reach later stages in life do they see marriage as contributing to an increased general state of happiness. Younger African American women, on the other hand, have greater expectations about marriage than younger African American men do. They view marriage as potentially improving their standard of living, their freedom, their emotional security, their sex lives, and their relations with parents and friends.

By their mid-thirties, though, African American women's level of expectations about marriage change. They no longer have high expectations about the capacity of marriage to increase their general state of happiness.

---

[10]Patterson, *Rituals of Blood,* 63–64.

[11]Shirley J. Hatchett, "Women and Men," in *Life in Black America,* ed. James S. Jackson (Newbury Park, Calif.: Sage Publications, 1991), 84–104.

[12]Scott J. South, "For Love or Money? Sociodemographic Determinants of the Expected Benefits from Marriage," in *The Changing American Family: Sociological and Demographic Perspectives,* ed. Scott J. South and Stewart E. Tolnay (Boulder, Colo.: Westview Press, 1992), 171–94.

It seems that by the time African American women reach their thirties, their improved standard of living relative to African American men makes marriage less necessary to meet their earlier expectations for instrumental and security awards from marriage. This, coupled with the fact that African American men are reticent to marry earlier on in the life cycle, makes for an emotional/life cycle dynamic in which African American men and women at every stage of their adult lives are moving away from marrying one another related to disillusionment about the perceived benefits of marriage.

Family of Origin

When we look at the data regarding family of origin and its relationship to African American marriages, a surprising dynamic reveals itself. Growing up in a single-parent household has no effect on African Americans' ever marrying. However, growing up in a household with two biological parents *reduces* the odds of ever marrying for African American women. Conversely, for African American boys, growing up in a household with both biological parents *increases* the odds of ever marrying 2.8 times. How do we explain this phenomenon? Patterson speculates that the conflict that was identified earlier in this discussion about gender relationships in the African American community results in many marriages where conflict remains a prevalent dynamic in the family system. If the parents decide to remain together, the impact on the female child may be to make her cautious about entering into a marital relationship where the same kind of conflict and bickering will occur.

Why does this not ring true for African American boys? Patterson believes that the strong effects of a paternal presence in the family counters the negative impact of the parental conflict. Patterson goes on to surmise:

> If the main source of the conflict is the father's philandering or abuse of the mother (as is often the case), this is likely to have a more crushing effect on the daughter's propensity to marry than on the son's. The girl identifies with her mother and is mortified by her father's behavior, taking it as a warning to be wary of marriage. The boy identifies with his father and comes to accept his behavior as the way men and husbands behave. He may even interpret his father's perseverance in the marriage as a strong signal that "real" men not only get married, but stay married, even if it means putting the wife in her place from time to time. The result is that the odds of ever being married are increased more than two and three quarters times. But accompanying these odds is an equally increased propensity to replicate the father's marital behavior.[13]

---

[13]Patterson, *Rituals of Blood,* 79.

As low as the marriage rates are for African Americans, the dissolution of marriage rate is proportionately higher. **Figure** 4 indicates that the marital disruption rate for African Americans is twice that of Latinos and almost three times that of European Americans. Patterson looked at a number of issues that might explain the high rates of marriage disruption, including age at marriage, sexual experience, demography, premarital behavior, family of origin, religiosity, attitudes about infidelity, attitudes about gender roles and responsibilities, and sexual attitudes and practices. Again, the structural features offered some insight, but did not carry sufficient weight to explain the dramatic differences that exist between African Americans and Americans in general. Nor were there overwhelming differences in

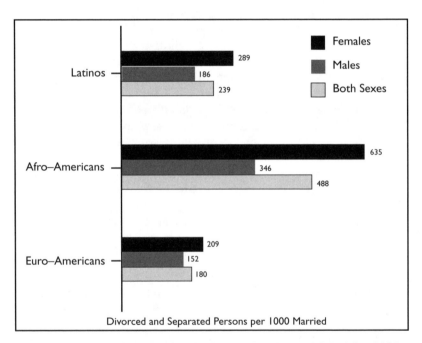

FIGURE 4: Marital Disruption Ratios, by Gender and Ethnicity, 1995

attitudes about gender roles and responsibilities that would account for the marital dissolution gap. However, in the case of sexual attitudes and practices the divergent perspectives among African American men and women were startling.

The differences can be put into four categories: (1) fundamental gender disagreements concerning sexual morality, (2) serious mismatch of preferences regarding sexual practices, (3) differences in level of sexual activity, and (4) sexual infidelity.

Regarding premarital sex, 25 percent of African American men think it is wrong, mirroring the percentage of other American men. Thirty-eight percent of African American women think premarital sex is wrong, compared with 30 percent of European American women. And 28 percent of the African American women who think premarital sex is wrong think that it is always wrong. When the religiosity of African American women is brought into play (i.e., those African American women who attend church on a weekly basis), the disapproval rate increases by a whopping 490 percent.

When it comes to sexual practices, African American men and women are fairly compatible in their dislike for anal sex and cunnilingus. However, in the case of fellatio, group sex, and sex with a stranger, huge differences emerge in preference for these sexual practices. For those sexual practices the percentage of African American men who like them is at least double that of African American women who do. In light of the fact that the percentages for "neither likes" is high on group sex and sex with a stranger, there is probably less conflict over those sexual practices than there is with fellatio, where the percentage of men who like fellatio is higher than either "neither likes" and "both dislike."

Regarding the number of sexual partners in the previous year, African American men have the lowest percentage of all groups when it comes to one partner and the highest percentage when it comes to two to three partners and more than three partners. Of those African Americans who have had three or more partners, men outnumber women by more than three to one. Granted, the majority (54 percent) of African American men have had only one partner. However, for African American women the number is 64 percent. In addition, the gender difference between European Americans is not nearly as large when it comes to two to three and more than three partners.

All these differences, though, pale in the face of the issue of infidelity. Eighty-three percent of married African American women reported that they had been faithful in their marriages (compared with 85 percent of European American women). Only 57 percent of married African American men reported that they had been faithful. Standing alone, perhaps each of these problems related to sexual attitudes, practices, and behaviors would not have as much impact on the African American community as they do. However, together the impact is devastating. Moreover, beyond the lowest marriage rates and the highest divorce rates, the concomitant problems of black father absence, the feminization of poverty, and the alienation of the genders has made it more difficult for African Americans to create households and neighborhoods that engender a sense of home.

These statistics from Patterson's research make it more clear why pastoral theologians such as Carroll Watkins Ali, Lee Butler, and Edward

Wimberly are writing the books they are writing. Watkins Ali sees the disruption occurring in African American families and worries whether or not the transmittal of a cultural heritage and tradition will survive.[14] If African American men and women cannot come together to create families of stability and continuity, then the cultural heritage and tradition that has been so crucial for a people's survival will be lost. A fragmented people results in a lost tradition. In light of the Patterson research we can better understand Butler's focus on the need to unite sexuality and spirituality in the pastoral care of African American marriages and families. He argues that a spirituality of sexuality needs to be revised within the African American community.

Spirituality of Sexuality

Butler points to how the ravages of racism have resulted in distorted images of the self for black people. Black bodies, sexually and otherwise physically abused, were the objects of repeated aggression during slavery. The black body was a symbol of that which was considered negative, base, and a threat to "purity."[15] Sexuality as a physical function of the body has been for many blacks the locale for the joining of the shame and negative self-image from the past with the act of procreation and sexual gratification. Consequently, from generation to generation African Americans have been passing on a sexual identity that challenges a sense of dignity. The spirituality that Butler recommends that blacks bring to their sexuality is one that recognizes sexuality as a good gift from God. And through lovingly shared sexuality black men and black women can affirm, care, nurture, and respect one another.

Sexuality linked with a redemptive spirituality, then, becomes the vehicle through which African Americans can begin to counter negative self-images and gender alienation. Blacks can also discern in the information about poor gender relationships the genesis of the increasing numbers of relational refugees identified by Wimberly. With so many unpartnered African Americans due to low marriage rates, high divorce rates, and divergent viewpoints on sexual attitudes and practices, relational refugeeism is a real and present threat to the communality of African American people.

Class Alienation

But gender alienation is not the only form of disconnectedness in the African American community at the beginning of the twenty-first century. Class divisions also make blacks a disconnected people. Class divisions are not new to the African American community. Ever since the distinctions

---

[14]Carroll Watkins Ali, *Survival and Liberation: Pastoral Theology in African American Context* (St. Louis: Chalice Press, 1999).

[15]Robert E. Hood, *Begrimed and Black: Christian Traditions on Blacks and Blackness* (Minneapolis: Fortress Press, 1994).

made in slavery between field niggers and house niggers, there has been some form of categorizing African Americans along the indices of income, type of job, education, and family connection. What is new today is an uneasiness in the African American community about the meaning of these class distinctions and what, if anything, should be done about them.

From slavery up until the turn of the twentieth century just about all African Americans were viewed as a single socioeconomic class. Class is not even the best word to describe how the larger society viewed blacks. In slavery, whether one worked in the big house or in the field, one was still a slave. You were owned by a slave master who had the power to determine just about all aspects of your life. After emancipation blacks were free but still remained a monolithic group, both in terms of limited civil rights and privileges and narrowly defined parameters of housing, income, jobs, and so on. That is, Jim Crow discrimination limited the range of possibilities when it came to where one could live, salaries, and what jobs were available. Such restrictions forced all African Americans into a constricted set of socioeconomic indices that was so narrow that little if any "class" difference seemed to exist. Yes, there were some doctors, attorneys, and educators who might claim a higher social status, but for the most part all African Americans shared the same social status. It wasn't until the twentieth century that sharper class distinctions among African Americans began to appear. Just at the turn of the twentieth century the distinctions took on not only economic and vocational dimensions but also a role in the uplift of the race dimensions.

The "debate" between W. E. B. DuBois and Booker T. Washington was, in part, a struggle between two class perspectives. DuBois, representing an educated "upper" class, proposed that this class take on a leadership role in determining the direction of African Americans. This talented tenth would act as role models and an inspiration for those in the "lower" classes, fighting for their civil rights in the larger American society. Washington, representing a "worker/farmer" class, encouraged African Americans to think less politically. His focus was to rally a people around collective self-sufficiency and independence. Political power would develop later from self-sufficiency and independence.

These differing viewpoints reflected the emergence of increased distinctions in socioeconomic stratification in the black community. By the 1940s the African American dream was so linked to the American dream of upward social mobility that the appearance of E. Franklin Frazier's *Black Bourgeoisie* met with great fanfare. The fact that a black bourgeoisie, with its own standards of inclusion and demarcation, could be defined seemed to herald that African Americans could live the American dream and that, in fact, some were doing so. From the 1950s to the 1970s African Americans could be found all along the social class spectrum, from lower class to upper class. African Americans were disproportionately represented at the lower end and disproportionately underrepresented at the upper levels. Yet African Americans were not distinguishable from the rest of Americans in that they held places along the social class continuum.

In the 1970s social scientists recognized that a different and disturbing development was occurring. First, there was a new social class category: the underclass. These were persons whose lack of participation in the ordinary activities of the larger society did not provide indicators that would place them in one class or another. Largely unemployed and unskilled, they did not have income, job, education, and other identifying features that determined class. And without these identifying marks they were not even to be placed on the class chart; they were relegated to a place "off" the chart—underclass.

Another distinguishing and disturbing feature of the appearance of the underclass was that the underclass phenomenon did not seem to work under the same principles as the other classes. The underclass did not appear to be aspiring to achieve a position higher up on the class ladder. Rather, underclass seemed to be a permanent class. Hopeless and despairing, this new group of mostly black urban poor, in response to disappearing prospects for an improved life, lived in a new world increasingly cut off from the rest of society.

A third dimension of this underclass phenomenon is the rapidity with which this group is growing. Not only are they a sizeable number of African Americans, their number is growing faster than that of African Americans with means. Consequently there is a rapidly growing gap between those who have been able to achieve a modicum of economic success and those who are stuck in poverty.

It is this reality that has most disturbed some pastoral theologians and womanist ethicists. When African Americans, no matter what their class, all lived in the same neighborhood, attended the same schools, worked side by side in their own businesses, and worshiped together, there was less of a chance for a large segment of the community to drift into oblivion. Yes, I acknowledge that times are different and that there is no turning back to a "golden age" of black utopian community. Moreover, I recognize that individual persons bear the bulk of the responsibility for how they lead their lives, stacked decks and limited resources notwithstanding. "Every tub has to sit on its own bottom," as my grandmother would say. Yet there is an ethical norm that exists in Christianity and other religions as well that confronts us with the fact that we are our neighbor's keeper.

As I stated in chapter 1, Joshua is not the only story that can be conjured in order to address the plight of African Americans in the current crisis. A story in the Midrash also speaks to the need for group solidarity. The ancient Israelites are fleeing for their lives from an enemy that is in hot pursuit. Those at the rear are those who are unable to keep up: children, elderly, and the disabled, whose position at the rear makes them the most vulnerable of all. In the end those at the rear are slaughtered. The story goes on to recount the anger that God has for those who went ahead, saving themselves and selfishly ignoring the plight of those at the rear.

It is those who are in the vulnerable position of the rear, the underclass, that Marcia Y. Riggs, Cheryl Sanders, and Emilie M. Townes are writing about. Each of them is issuing a call to African Americans who are more affluent to pay attention to those of our brothers and sisters who are most at risk in this society.

Who are they? They principally are our children up to the age of twenty-five. As infants they have the highest mortality rate. Growing up, six in ten of them live in poverty. One in four does not have a father present in the household. As teenagers they have the highest suicide rate among all teens. Homicide is the number one cause of death for young African American men between the ages of eighteen and twenty-five. It is African American children and young adults who are most harshly impacted by the world of the urban poor.

Joshua and Connectedness

In chapter 1, I highlighted the themes of promise, fulfillment, and guarantee as central to the Joshua story. In this chapter, which addresses the topics of connectedness and disconnectedness among African Americans, I want to lift up the subthemes of loyalty, commitment, accountability, and sacrifice. It is through the virtues of loyalty, commitment, sacrifice, and accountability that African Americans can begin to become a more connected people. For African Americans to participate in the promise, fulfillment, and guarantee of God, they must exhibit the virtues of loyalty, commitment, sacrifice, and accountability.

The loyalty and commitment I am encouraging is multifaceted and integrated. It is loyalty and commitment to God, to common goals, and to one another. This kind of loyalty and commitment are crucial ingredients of a people being connected to one another.

Another important dimension of connectedness is self-sacrifice. All meaningful and successful relationships require some self-sacrifice on the part of the participants. Some willingness to forgo one's own interests, to compromise, to relinquish control is necessary in order for the relationship to persist. Without this the emotional scale of the relationship is unbalanced, leading to feelings of mistrust and resentment. When there is sacrifice on both sides, persons not only feel supported in the relationship but also feel that the relationship itself has a future; that is, there is hope that they can stay connected. Loyalty, commitment, and sacrifice are virtues that must be instituted in a relationship. They do not just happen. Persons must take responsibility to ensure that the loyalty, commitment, and sacrifice are there. Thus, relationships require accountability.

Accountability is the ethical power source that helps ensure that relationships maintain their continuity and viability. Accountability is the fuel that drives persons to want to "do the right thing," to do the necessary things in order to stay connected. Accountability spurs persons to acknowledge when they are not doing their part *and* to commit to do differently.

Loyalty, commitment, sacrifice, and accountability inseparably make up the whole cloth of connectedness. To be connected to another or others certainly can include other things, such as empathy, respect, and trust. The items of loyalty, commitment, sacrifice, and accountability are not an all-inclusive list of what connectedness comprises. However, as we turn to the story of Joshua, these four virtues stand out as chief ingredients in the successful campaign of the ancient Israelites to establish a home for themselves.

Loyalty in Joshua operates in three different realms: (1) loyalty between God and the ancient Israelites, (2) loyalty to a common mission on the part of God and the ancient Israelites, and (3) loyalty among the ancient Israelites.

God's loyalty to the ancient Israelites is embedded in God's promise that was made to Abraham and then reaffirmed with Moses. "Every place that the sole of your foot will tread upon I have given to you, as I promised to Moses…No one shall be able to stand against you all the days of your life. As I was with Moses, so I will be with you; I will not fail you or forsake you" (Josh. 1:3, 5). The Joshua conquest is a continuation of God's ongoing commitment to establish a home for Abraham and his descendants, which was renewed in the deliverance of the ancient Israelites from Egypt. God remains loyal to this promise that was made centuries ago. God's loyalty in Joshua is God making good on the covenantal promises made to Abraham in Genesis 17:8–"And I will give to you, and to your offspring after you, the land where you are now an alien, all the land of Canaan, for a perpetual holding; and I will be their God"–and to Moses in Exodus 3:7–8:

> Then the LORD said, "I have observed the misery of my people who are in Egypt; I have heard their cry on account of their taskmasters. Indeed, I know their sufferings, and I have come down to deliver them from the Egyptians, and to bring them up out of that land to a good and broad land, a land flowing with milk and honey, to the country of the Canaanites, the Hittites, the Amorites, the Perizzites, the Hivites, and the Jebusites.

Joshua bears witness to the loyalty of God as a promise-keeping God. Throughout the book of Joshua, God loyally directs resources and empowers the ancient Israelites in their conquest of the land. But covenantal loyalty applies both to God and to the Israelites.

The loyalty of God is embedded in the covenant that God made with the ancient Israelites that God would be their God if they would be God's people. Therefore, the loyalty of God to be God's people is to be mirrored by the people in their loyalty to God. Joshua 1:6–9 describes, from God's point of view, how the Israelites are to demonstrate their loyalty. They are to "be strong and courageous" and adhere to the law of Moses. If the ancient Israelites will be loyal in this way, then God will be with them wherever they go. In addition, God stipulates that no spoils should be taken from the cities that were overtaken. Achan was not loyal to this provision, and as a result God did not honor God's side of the covenant. At Ai the ancient Israelites were defeated because of their disloyalty. The lesson that we learn from Joshua is that loyalty fosters the benefits of connectedness, and disloyalty leads to the harmful consequences associated with disconnectedness. Loyalty that is mutually shared fosters greater connectedness and commitment on the part of both parties. When loyalty is either absent or betrayed, it not only harms but also diminishes a sense of connectedness and commitment. Remaining loyal to the commitments that they make to one another empowers persons to remain connected.

Before there is loyalty, there is commitment. That is, loyalty is the follow-through and follow-up on commitment. Commitment is both the initial pledge and the overarching desire to link one's destiny with that of another person, persons, or institution. A person can also be committed to an idea or a movement. Whatever the object of the commitment, the one who makes the commitment ties his or her future to that to which a commitment has been made. Commitments usually take on a concrete structure or form. That is, the commitment is to do something, or be something in relationship to the other. In marriage the partners make a commitment to love, cherish, respect, and be faithful to each other. Their loyalty to that commitment means that the initial commitment made on the wedding day carries through for the rest of their lives. Loyalty is commitment preserved over time.

There is a dynamic in the notions of commitment and loyalty that becomes most prevalent when the relationship is experiencing difficulty. The difficulty could be external, such as a natural disaster, loss of a loved one, or a layoff. Or the difficulty could be internal to the relationship itself, such as a difference of opinion, betrayal, or loss of affection. In either case the commitment is jeopardized. The persons who have made a previous commitment to each other may no longer feel, or feel as strongly, that they want to cast their destiny with the other. Their future together seems less sure and guaranteed. Loyalty to the earlier commitment means that in spite of difficulty, persons make the effort to maintain the earlier commitment.

Now loyalty does not necessarily mean that the relationship will inevitably remain intact. A decision may be made to sever the relationship and thereby rescind the previous commitment. However, the loyalty to a committed relationship means that the persons will do all that they can to sustain their commitment. The commitment is not to be taken lightly. Loyalty within commitments drives persons to exert maximum effort to see how the earlier commitment can be sustained even in the midst of difficulty and challenges to its fulfillment.

The Joshua story is full of mini-stories about commitment and loyalty. Rahab and the spies make commitments to one another that they loyally keep. The Transjordan tribes make a commitment to Moses to fight with the Canaanite Israelites in the conquest of the land. In loyalty to their earlier commitment they do battle alongside the other tribes before going back across the Jordan. In loyalty to a commitment made in Deuteronomy 20:5–16, the ancient Israelites spare the Gibeonites even though the Gibeonites deceived them by disguising themselves as from a far away land. Perhaps the best example of loyalty sustaining commitment in the face of internal conflict is the story of reconciliation that takes place between the Canaanite Israelites and the Transjordan tribes.

Throughout the campaign to reclaim their inheritance, the Transjordan tribes loyally follow through on the commitment that they had made to Moses and then renewed with Joshua. They would help the other tribes secure Canaan before returning to their inheritance across the Jordan. On their way back they build an altar of remembrance, which is interpreted by the Canaanite Israelites as a sign of renunciation of affiliation. In fact, the altar is a symbol of remembrance. Many of the Canaanite Israelites want to do battle with the Transjordan tribes because of the perceived insult of building an altar for sacrifice outside the Deuternomically prescribed central sanctuary (Deut. 12:13–14). Representatives from the Canaanite tribes are sent to the Reubenites, Gadites, and half-tribe of Manasseh to confront them about their behavior. In the ensuing conversation the Transjordan tribes are able to explain their intent in building an altar, explaining that they have no intent of being disloyal either to God or to the other Israelites. In the face of perceived disloyalty, the loyalty of the ancient Israelites toward one another averts a war between them.

Remaining loyal to a previously made commitment often involves sacrifice in order to remain connected. The need to forgo one's own agenda, interests, and priorities is a necessary ingredient in any relationship where persons want to remain connected to each other. In a relationship it is impossible for persons to expect that they will always agree. Too much agreement is a sign either of one person completely capitulating to the other or a symbiotic merger in which two persons have become one. Although such an arrangement eliminates conflict, it also eliminates the presence of two whole persons in a relationship. The sacrifice in a relationship should never be all on one side. Instead, it should be as balanced as possible. At any given moment there may be more sacrifice on one side than the other, but the tipping of the scales, if it does have to happen, should go back and forth.

The reason why persons are willing and need to sacrifice in order to remain connected is that in a relationship three parties are present: the individual parties, as well as the relationship that exists between them. In order to preserve the relationship and its goals, it is necessary for the individual parties to sacrifice their individual agendas.

This is a major theme in Joshua. A commitment to the people and their campaign to reclaim their inheritance requires that individual persons and tribes sacrifice, for the time being, their own individual interests. When this happens, the resulting outcome benefits not only the whole but also the individual parties. When sacrifice does not occur, both the larger enterprise and individuals suffer. In the case of Achan his individual greed and inability to sacrifice resulted in defeat for the ancient Israelites as a whole, as well as eventual death for himself. The Transjordan tribes, who were able to sacrifice immediate acquisition of their land, contributed to the successful conquest of Canaan, as well as eventual acquisition of land for themselves across the Jordan.

In order for connectedness to be fully realized, accountability has to be included along with commitment, loyalty, and sacrifice. Accountability recognizes that in light of the commitment that has been made, one is responsible for maintaining that commitment with loyalty and sacrifice. Not only does accountability apply to doing what needs doing in order to honor the commitment, it also requires that in light of one's failure to do what needs to be done, there needs to be a renewed commitment to do so.

Thus, I make a distinction between responsibility and accountability. Accountability is a willingness to accept responsibility. Too often in our contemporary society we understand responsibility and accountability to be the same thing. Responsibility is being able to respond to the demands that a commitment makes upon a person. If one wants to be in a connected relationship, one has the responsibility to be loyal and to sacrifice, among other things. If one does not do those things, one is not being responsible. Accountability includes responsibility (doing what needs to be done), but calls for more. Accountability requires that when responsibility wanes, there needs to be a redoubling of efforts to restore the commitment.

Another way of talking about the distinction I am trying to make is to say that there are two aspects of responsibility. There is a responsibility that does what is right (does what is needed), but there also is a responsibility that makes things right (seeks restoration). Accountability makes sure that responsibility is maintained. In Joshua the best example of accountability is found in chapter 24, when Joshua asks the tribes whether or not they will remain loyal in their commitment to Yahweh as their God. Joshua pledges his loyalty: "But as for me and my household, we will serve the LORD" (Josh. 24:15). And when the people pledge their loyalty, Joshua warns them that the Lord will hold them to their commitment. When the people again pledge their loyalty, Joshua tells them, "You are witnesses against yourselves that you have chosen the LORD, to serve him" (24:2).

Joshua then sets up a stone under an oak and says, "See, this stone shall be a witness against us; for it has heard all the words of the LORD that he spoke to us; therefore it shall be a witness against you, if you deal falsely with your God" (24:27). The ancient Israelites make themselves accountable to the covenant that they have made with God. Their connectedness to God was not to be a one-time event, but to be perpetual, as long-lasting as the stone. Every time the people strayed from their commitment, the stone was to be a reminder to them (a witness against them) that they had strayed and needed to restore the covenantal commitment they had made. Connectedness in Joshua calls for accountability to commitment that promises to renew the commitment when it falters.

The kind of connectedness that is represented in Joshua is the kind of connectedness that is needed in the African American community today. The alienation and conflict that exist, especially among adult men and women, threatens the viability of family life in the African American community. Strong, stable, reliable, consistent, and trustworthy family systems are necessary for the well-being of adults and children. Without them African Americans are much more vulnerable to poverty, illness, and hopelessness. We seem to be giving up on the idea of being connected as a people. Disappointment and betrayal seem to be the primary culprits.

Can African Americans find a way of reclaiming a connectedness to one another such that the disappointment and betrayal can be overcome? And can the black church play a role in this recovery of a home for black couples and families? I think so, but the black church and its leadership have a monumental task in front of them, because the black church itself has not always dealt forthrightly with difficult issues in African American gender relationships.

If, as Patterson has revealed, infidelity is the chief problem in African American gender relationships, the black church must step forward and address the issue. The black church must provide a clear and unambiguous message that fidelity in marriage is the expected norm. Not only is fidelity in marriage a commitment made in the wedding ceremony, but also fidelity in marriage ensures the greater well-being of the African American community. The truth of the matter is that the admonition against infidelity is most appropriately directed toward African American men. It is their attitudes about sex outside of marriage that primarily contribute to the low marriage rates, high divorce rates, and father absence in the black community. Again, it needs to be said that the vast majority of black men are faithful husbands. However, the declining marriage rate and increasing divorce rate are placing the African American community in increasing danger for physical, emotional, and spiritual disease. As the sacred institution that helps establish the earthly institution of marriage, the church has the responsibility to help ensure the "benefits" of marriage for the men, women, and children who constitute African American families.

And here is where the black male leadership in the African American church is most open to criticism. The criticism is twofold: (1) African American pastoral leaders have not always modeled the fidelity that the church preaches and teaches, and (2) the infidelities of black leaders place the African American community in a dilemma. Because African Americans are a people who were uprooted from their African homeland and brought to a place that was not their own, they have historically looked to leadership to interpret and guide their existence in an alien place. In the past these religious leaders, most often men, have played a bigger-than-life role in the salvation of blacks in America.[16] Today African Americans still look to those leaders who will give meaning and guidance to the ongoing struggle to survive. When black preachers take advantage of those who have been entrusted to their care, they not only betray a trust but also give sanction to abuse. Black clergy sexual abuse helps reinforce a message that infidelity and lack of responsibility are normative in their community. The black community needs fewer "players" (as in play the field) and more "stayers" (as in stay at home). A Joshua church fosters the virtues of commitment, sacrifice, responsibility, and accountability among all its members.

At those times when black clergy betray trust through sexual misconduct, the black community is placed in a conundrum. The dilemma is to either ignore the immorality of the acts in order to give "support" to the movement and its leaders or to condemn the leader's behavior and thereby undercut the leader's authority. Blacks either have to forgo any moral standards in the community in order to show support for their leadership or castigate their leadership on moral grounds, which diminishes the leader's status as leader. Now the argument could be made that this dilemma is not a real one; rather, it is a dilemma fabricated by the media. Accurate though that perspective may be, the fact of the matter is that African Americans should not be put in a position where they have to in any way defend or make allowances for behavior that contributes to African American disconnectedness. And the best deterrent to any unwanted rituals of accountability for wrongful acts is the preventive acts of commitment, sacrifice, and responsible behavior.

In addition to its leadership putting its own house in order, the black church can intervene in a variety of ways to stem the tide of African American disconnectedness.

Premarital counseling. No couple getting married in a black church should be married without premarital counseling; no counseling, no wedding. And

---

[16]Charles V. Hamilton, *The Black Preacher in America* (New York: Morrow, 1972).

a principal topic for discussion in addition to finances, children, in-laws, resolving arguments, communication, and so on, is the issue of fidelity in marriage. Now this may seem somewhat harsh and draconian. However, the current level of pain and hardship caused by infidelity in African American marriages and families requires drastic action. Moreover, in the premarital counseling there should be ample time for the discussion of sexual practices and preferences. Couples should be helped early on to know what each other wants regarding sexual activity. Questions regarding the frequency of sex and the kinds of sexual activity desired should be talked about openly and fully. Even if a couple has already been engaged in sexual activity, there may be issues surrounding their current sexual practices and preferences that need sorting out.

Five-year relational reviews. It would be a good idea if pastors were to have a review of the relationship with couples every five years. This relational "checkup" would focus on the same topics covered in premarital counseling. The intent would be to see if there are any areas of conflict or tension that have arisen. Such a review would address the signs and presence of disconnectedness that might be appearing. In this way the review could be both preventive and curative, reinforcing the things that the couple is doing well to remain connected and addressing the start of any problems.

Religious education. Bible classes or topical classes on the issues that promote connectedness would be a powerful asset to the ministry of any church that wanted to strengthen African American marriages and families. The classes should probably not be on the subject of fidelity in marriage, but on the issues that underlie strong, intact marriages: good communication, mutual regard and respect, effective conflict resolution, balancing care for self and care of the other, and so on. Such classes could be offered to a variety of different groups: couples, men, women, married men, married women, single men, and single women. Discussion around a particular book might be a helpful way of getting into the issues.

Mentoring programs. For African American children who are in danger of becoming relational refugees, a mentoring relationship is a way of helping them remain connected. Notice that I did not say children from single-parent homes. In some cases the alienation from both biological parents or a stepparent has resulted in a child's detachment from meaningful adult guidance. Mentoring programs can be set up as one-on-one relationships between a mentor and a mentee or in the context of a fuller program of rites of passage and other structured activities. In either case the crucial dimension is the child's connection with an adult.

As a Joshua people pursue a home for themselves, the Joshua church needs to lift up those elements of a connected life together that make for successful claim on their inheritance. Commitment, loyalty, sacrifice, and accountability help guarantee the promise of survival and liberation. God has already provided a home for African Americans in which love and fulfillment are resident. The task for African American people is to live out the qualities necessary for a connected life and in so doing claim the promised inheritance.

CHAPTER 5

A Vision for the Future with Hope

The third feature of the African American campaign to reclaim an inheritance of full humanity is the appropriation of a vision for the future. Such a vision for the future describes that place where African Americans perceive the fulfillment of their destiny to lie. As has been stated earlier, such a place is not necessarily defined by geography, although there may be aspects of physical location associated with the hoped for place. Rather, the hoped for place is an intangible state of being variously defined as full humanity or cultural fulfillment. Such a place is defined less by external environment and more by internal attitudes and consciousness. The spiritual "Deep River" reflects this external/internal duality of place as it speaks of a promised land where all is peace:

> Deep River, my home is over Jordan.
> Deep River, I want to cross over into campground.
> Oh, don't you want to go to that Gospel feast;
> That Promised Land where all is peace.
>
> Deep River, my home is over Jordan.
> Deep River, I want to cross over into campground.

In this spiritual we hear the desire to be at a place other than where one is at now. The desire is to be home, and the present location is not home. Home is over Jordan. And that home is a campground of praise, a gospel feast, a promised land, and a place of peace. The solemn cadence with which this spiritual is usually sung echoes not just a desire but a deep longing for all that lies across the Jordan. It is a vision rich with images of all that makes for a home of wholeness and fulfillment. But the vision of the future presented in "Deep River" is rich in other ways as well.

A full vision for the future not only describes the desired place but also points in the direction of where the desired place lies. In the spiritual the place of promise is over Jordan. The vision not only indicates what is desired but also reveals in what direction one has to travel in order to arrive at the desired place. Visions that give direction are more powerful, because they show that it is possible to get from here to there. Magical places that exist in some never-never land, whose approximate relationship to the present location is unclear, seem more removed and unattainable. If one wanted to go there, where would one go; what direction would one take? Unable to see the way there, the desired destination forever remains an impossible dream.

The spiritual "Deep River" reveals one other thing in its vision of a future home: There is a river to cross in order to get there. Those who wish to arrive in that promised land of peace must traverse a river, a deep river, whose symbolic meaning suggests struggle, courage, and determination. The vision of the future in "Deep River" is a complete vision, for it not only describes the desired place but also shows what direction must be taken and what will be required to get there. African Americans today need such a complete vision. Some in the African American community have begun this task of vision creation.

National Public Radio talk show host Tavis Smiley has compiled a collection of statements from widely known African Americans titled *How to Make Black America Better.*[1] Each of the twenty-eight writers presents his or her vision for the future. Each of these visions is attempting to describe a different and better place for African Americans. As the title indicates, the emphasis in the book is on how to get to this better place. Smiley himself makes ten recommendations:

1. Think black first, 100 percent of the time.

2. Look past what whites are doing to us to see what we are doing to ourselves.

3. Every Black American should put family first.

4. Black Americans must consider the consequences of their actions.

5. Every Black American should see him- or herself as part of a larger Black community.

---

[1]Tavis Smiley, ed., *How to Make Black America Better: Leading African Americans Speak Out* (New York: Doubleday, 2001).

6. Every Black American must preserve his or her health—physically, emotionally, psychologically, and spiritually.

7. Every Black American should develop an economic plan.

8. Make education the number one priority for every Black American.

9. Encourage the Black Church to do more.

10. Every Black American should establish a Black American legacy.[2]

In Smiley's and the other contributors' statements are echoes of some of the points presented in previous chapters of this book that reinforce the idea that a vision for the future for African Americans is linked to issues of cultural identity and connectedness.

> The ultimate effectiveness (power) of any group of people is the degree to which they have an awareness of who they are and respect for themselves. –Na'im Akbar[3]

> Our only hope as African Americans in this hostile world is to march, work, and strive *together*. –Earl G. Graves[4]

> One of the things that must happen in our community, as we advance into a new century and especially a new millennium, is a renewed commitment…a commitment to our families, others, and ourselves. –Shaquille O'Neal[5]

But something important has been lost as we have thrown away or traded so much of our black spiritual heritage for a false sense of economic security and inclusion.

> What can we do? We must begin by insisting that the promise to leave no child behind in our country really means something, and we must hold everyone who makes this promise accountable. In the Black community, we must learn to reweave the rich fabric of community for our children and to reinstill the values and sense of purpose our elders and mentors have always embraced. –Marian Wright Edelman[6]

---

[2]Ibid., 5–39.

[3]Na'im Akbar, "Making Black America Better Through Self-Knowledge," in Smiley, *How to Make Black America Better,* 133.

[4]Earl G. Graves, "Leveraging Our Power," in Smiley, *How to Make Black America Better,* 107.

[5]Shaquille O'Neal, "Behaving Better," in Smiley, *How to Make Black America Better,* 113.

[6]Marian Wright Edelman, "What We Can Do," in Smiley, *How to Make Black America Better,* 121–22.

As Akbar, Graves, O'Neal, and Edelman describe the means for achieving the goal for the future (making black America better), they are simultaneously describing the goal itself. If African Americans can possess a self-awareness of and respect for themselves, then that awareness and respect will come alive and become a people's power. When African Americans march, work, and strive together, hope lives. In committing themselves to their families, others, and one another, African Americans generate the commitment to create a new thing in the new millennium. If African Americans make themselves accountable to the notion that no child will be left behind, no child will be left behind. Reweaving the fabric of African American community reestablishes the values and sense of purpose rooted in the African American traditions of the past.

In the Joshua story the accomplished acquisition of the promised land is rooted in the action of acquiring. The same is true for African Americans: as African Americans strive to make black America better, black America becomes better. The promise of a better black America is fulfilled in the living out of the belief that the promise has been fulfilled. Engaging in the struggle to claim full humanity is to achieve full humanity; the promise is fulfilled by living into the fulfilled promise.

This is why Farah Jasmine Griffin's question is so important: "Who set you flowin?" Just entering into the divinely ordained enterprise guarantees a successful outcome. Who will set African Americans "flowin" today? Is there an idea, a project, a cause, an event, or series of events that will get us to enter into the waters of the Jordan and thereby not only claim but achieve our inheritance?

Reparations

One of the projects that has gained substantial attention recently has been the call for reparations. Reparations has been identified as a strategy for stemming the negative effects of slavery and producing a more hopeful future for African Americans. Could the campaign for reparations for African Americans be a vision that empowers a people to cross over Jordan into the promised land?

Reparations for African Americans is repayment of a debt owed to African Americans by the United States. The growth and development of the United States as a wealthy and prosperous nation were due in large measure to the free labor forced from enslaved Africans who were brought to America against their will. Slavery and its subsequent variations of Jim Crow discrimination and civil rights violations have contributed to the languishing African Americans suffer compared with whites in a variety of ways—economically, psychologically, educationally, and politically. The cost to African Americans has been great. Affirmative action is a well-meaning effort to help make up the debt owed to African Americans, but it is only a miniscule payment compared with the enormity of the harm that has been done. African Americans have a claim on the United States to pay its debt and thereby bear its responsibility in helping to bring African Americans to full humanity and fulfillment.

Proponents of reparations argue that when African Americans are fully compensated for their labor and the costs of slavery, they might be able to fashion for themselves a home in America. Such a home would not only provide full opportunity but also full parity with whites. In this different kind of home the minority status of African Americans in terms of numbers would be protected from the political tyranny of the majority. In this home more, not fewer, young black men would be enrolled in college than in the criminal justice system. Young single black women with children would no longer be the largest segment of the population living in poverty. In this larger collective home there would be more homes with intact families. Higher marriage rates and lower divorce rates would establish stable families that provide nurturing and loving homes for children and a strong social network to sustain African American culture and heritage. African Americans would no longer feel the need to be apologetic or feel the need to prove themselves, for there would be full acknowledgment of the contributions they have made and continue to make to America. And finally, it would be a home where the history of slavery in America would no longer be a source of shame either for the descendants of enslaved Africans or for the descendants of slave owners but would act as a historical witness against America's current and future generations that enslavement of any kind violates God's promises and destiny for humankind. Such a home would indeed be a promised land. This vision of the promised land is not only a place to be desired (full compensation), but within it lies the path of how to get there (payment of the debt).

Do reparations—that is, payment of the debt owed—provide an adequate vision for the future for African Americans? That is, are reparations the path to the promised land described in the preceding paragraph? At this point the answer to that question is unclear for a number of reasons. For one thing, the full details of the debt repayment plan have not been outlined. The questions that remain include: (1) What resources and how much will it take to pay the debt (money, education, cultural and historical retrieval, political reform?) (2) How long will it take to pay the debt? (3) Where will the resources come from? (4) Who will monitor the payments and their effectiveness? The answers to these questions must be clarified in order to determine the viability of the reparations strategy. These questions will require substantial reflection and calculation in order for reparations to become a viable vision for African Americans for the future.

Person of faith though I am, I wonder how willing the United States will be to provide the resources needed to make up for slavery and the two-hundred-year cascade of its evil impact. In the past, America has been willing to let its citizens of color languish at the bottom of the socioeconomic ladder. Recent declines in these indices have gone largely unnoticed and misinterpreted. Welfare reform and attacks on affirmative action have alternatively been the cause and the response to worsening conditions for African Americans. The development of an underclass suggests that America is more likely to make more room at the bottom than at the top. In the past the United States has refused to apologize for the dirge of slavery. Can we expect the United States to pay a debt that it refuses to acknowledge?

An even larger problem with reparations is that reparations place African Americans in an almost exclusively dependent position when it comes to their survival and liberation. This is a vulnerable place for African Americans to voluntarily place themselves. Putting one's survival and liberation at the mercy and largesse of America is reminiscent of the slaves, whose life and well-being depended on the beneficence of the "good" slaveowner. Control remains in the hands of those paying the debt. What if America demands exclusive right to determine the kind and amount of reparations to be paid; what if America decides to pay back only a portion; what if in the payback process, America decides to renege on an earlier promise? African Americans would just have to accept what was done or not done. There would be no recourse, no capacity to make America do right. Reparations assume that without payment on the debt African Americans will be unable to thrive and overcome the negative impact of slavery. Do African Americans want to put themselves in a position where the future of their fate lies solely in the hands of America? Or should they place their fate in the hands of God, who guarantees to deliver on the promise of full humanity and fulfillment?

With the ideal vision of a home for African Americans and the introduction of reparations as a possible vehicle for the fulfillment of that vision, we turn to our conjure of Joshua for guidance and insight.

Joshua and a Vision for the Future

In Joshua the vision for the future for the ancient Israelites is the inheritance of the land that had been promised to them by God. The vision in Joshua is an extension of the vision presented in Exodus and Deuteronomy; a land flowing with milk and honey will be provided for a people who have been disinherited from their home and land. The path to the achievement of that vision is the courageous and determined struggle of a people to claim what has been promised to them. With God's guarantee and assistance the ancient Israelites secure a place for themselves, which becomes not only an occasion for the recovery of identity but also an opportunity to strengthen the connectedness among the tribes.

In many ways the vision for the future in Joshua is a recovery of the past that is then cast in a new manner for the future. That is, the future vision has at its core the stories, rituals, and symbols of the past. The culture and traditions of a people that have been forged in the past are brought forward to establish the fundamental parameters of a vision for the future.

The way forward entails a look back. The look back reminds the ancient Israelites of what has brought them safe thus far and has the potential to lead them home.

Nowhere is this theme stronger than in the final speech that Joshua delivers in chapter 24. In this farewell address at Shechem, Joshua recounts the history of God's faithfulness to the ancient Israelites as a precursor to his description of their future. Joshua connects the benefits of the present and future with the past deeds of God by reminding them of what they have because of God's intervention: "I gave you a land on which you had not labored, and towns thst you had not built, and you live in them; you eat the fruit of vineyards and oliveyards that you did not plant" (24:13). In essence Joshua is telling the people that their future destiny depends on their faithfulness to God. He reinforces this message with a warning that a lack of faithfulness in the future will result in tragedy: "If you forsake the LORD and serve foreign gods, then he will turn and do you harm, and consume you, after having done you good" (24:20). Joshua presents two possible scenarios for the future and challenges the people to choose between them. They choose the scenario that reflects their continued devotion to the God who has been with them in the past.

If, indeed, the vision for the future in Joshua is settlement in the land promised by God, what does such a life look like? What constitutes a life lived in the guarantee of God's past promises now fulfilled in the present? Or to ask the question in another way: what is life that is lived in full humanity with cultural fulfillment?

First, it is a life lived beyond mere survival. Prior to their entrance into Canaan the ancient Israelites lived as slaves and wanderers. In Egypt they had no destiny other than to exist in perpetual servitude. In the desert they eked out an existence that barely allowed them to arrive at the Jordan. In Canaan, however, the ancient Israelites establish a life for themselves that is guided by self-determination and purpose. No longer enslaved by the agenda of others or unsure about their destination, the ancient Israelites in Canaan begin to fashion a life of purpose and meaning that is more reflective of their freedom and power. They are free to answer to no one else but God. They are empowered to become more self-sufficient. In Canaan they possess a future that is more than mere survival. It is a life with a destiny and a life with the power to realize that destiny: full humanity.

The destiny of full humanity in Joshua includes the freedom to celebrate one's cultural identity, as well as the freedom to fully receive the gifts of life from God. This definition of full humanity is not exhaustive of all the features that could be associated with full humanity. They are, however, the two features of full humanity that present themselves most vividly in Joshua.

One of the more striking developments in the book of Joshua is the recovery of cultural heritage process, which occurs throughout the narrative. Sometimes the first step in the celebration of cultural identity is the recovery of a lost, stolen, or set aside cultural heritage and tradition. For forty years the ancient Israelites had wandered in the wilderness. During that time at least one, and we can suspect even more, of the rituals that formed Israelite cultural identity disappeared. The future vision for life in Canaan included the recovery and reestablishment of the cultural heritage of the ancient Israelites. A strong, healthy cultural identity was crucial for the conquest campaign and would be necessary for sustaining the settlement of the land. Recounting the history of the people in Joshua 24 was also a way in which the cultural heritage of the Israelites was conjured as a means for solidifying the cultural identity of the people. As cultural rituals and cultural heritage were recovered, repeated, and recited, the ancient Israelites reinforced their identity of who they were and whose they were, thereby strengthening their sense of full humanity.

A principal gift of life is the opportunity to live out one's life destiny. The story of Joshua is a declaration that the destiny of the Israelites is for them to live a life free from enslavement and free from aimless wandering. Their destiny is to secure a place where they can fulfill the promise declared by God to Abraham in Genesis 15. It is in that place where God has promised that they will grow, thrive, live secure, and find rest. And for a long time the ancient Israelites were able to live out their destiny because of the mutual faithfulness between God and the Joshua generation: "Israel served the LORD all the days of Joshua, and all the days of the elders who outlived Joshua and had known all the work that the LORD did for Israel" (24:31).

Joshua and Reparations

The campaign to reclaim the promised inheritance included reliance on material resources and the internalization of a renewed collective cultural identity. Neither by itself was sufficient to deliver on the promises of God. Without manna from heaven the ancient Israelites would have starved in the desert. Without weapons with which to fight the battles they would have been defeated. Clearly some forms of material goods were needed for victory. However, those material instruments were not enough. Internal qualities of faithfulness, courage, and commitment were also necessary to ensure victory. Achan's lack of faithfulness is a prime example of how important these intangible resources are in the struggle to achieve one's destiny. The difference between victory and defeat at Ai depended not on the amount of material resources but on the faithfulness of the ancient Israelites. When they remembered their heritage and held fast to their covenant with God, success was theirs.

I believe the same duality of assets (material resources and faithfulness) applies to the survival and liberation of African Americans. Materially, African Americans lag behind whites on a number of socioeconomic indices. A prolonged infusion of capital and material resources can certainly close the economic resources gap that exists between blacks and whites. And to the extent that capital and economic resources play a role in improved health, educational opportunities, and a higher quality of life, these material resources are crucial components to black survival and liberation. However, these resources alone do not guarantee the survival and liberation of a people. When it comes to marriage rates for African Americans, increased financial resources do not improve the chances of getting married. In fact, for African American adults increased financial resources are associated with decreased marriage rates. The argument can be made, then, that more important than the economic resources, the resources related to the internal consciousness raising of African Americans are what is needed for the achievement of full humanity. The material resources are not to be jettisoned, but alongside the material resources the internal consciousness resources are equally important, if not more so.

Randall Robinson argues similarly when he writes, "The issue here is not whether or not we can, or will, win reparations. The issue is whether we will fight for reparations because we have decided for ourselves that they are our due."[7] The recovery of an internal pride and sense of worth that would move African Americans to claim the debt owed is more important than the actual payment of the debt. Over the past three hundred years African Americans have been denied full access to the heritage and tradition that reflect their true cultural identity. During that same period African American families have had to endure the lingering effects of slavery's assault on African Americans' capacity to love and connect with one another. Money alone will not remedy these tragedies. What is needed more than money is the recovery of a sense of pride in a rich cultural history that predates Western civilization and that dramatically influenced the prosperity of the United States. What is needed is the increased sense of connectedness that enables African American men and women to love, commit, and provide loving, intact families for black children.

In Joshua the ancient Israelites do not request entrance into the lands they are to occupy. They assume that there will be opposition to their venture, so they thereby enter into a campaign to recover their inheritance without any expectation of cooperation on the other side. So, too, should African Americans carry out their campaign for reparations without the expectation that the United States will willingly honor its debt. Just as in the civil rights movement, where every freedom and right had to be fought for individually, battle by battle, so, too, in the campaign for reparations

---

[7]Randall N. Robinson, *The Debt: What America Owes Blacks* (New York: E. P. Dutton, 2000), 206.

there will have to be a prolonged battle to gain every portion of the debt owed. This will be a protracted campaign, with any number of different individual battles that will make up the whole. Not unlike the Underground Railroad of the nineteenth century, the journey home for African Americans in the twenty-first-century will be characterized by struggle. A primary struggle will be to get the United States to acknowledge that it has a debt to pay, let alone pay it. Another aspect of the struggle will be to find the most effective way of structuring debt payment so that it achieves the end that it seeks. Along the way there will be advances and setbacks. The advances are to be celebrated and lifted up to reinforce resolve. The setbacks will have to be responded to as occasions for learning rather than as excuses to abandon the debt payment plan.

The struggle will have to be adopted as a necessary and essential part of the process—there will be no easy way across this Jordan. The battle to work together will include intra- and intergroup debate. African Americans will have differing ideas about reparations and will struggle with one another about the best way to proceed. African Americans will certainly have to do battle with those who either oppose reparations or want to pay only partially on the debt owed. The time to rest as if the campaign is over has not arrived yet. There is still much for which African Americans must continue to fight in order to achieve full humanity and cultural fulfillment.

From the perspective of Joshua a primary focus of attention in the reparations campaign should be on the recovery of the history and heritage that have been downplayed and degraded in the American experience. The Joshua campaign of the ancient Israelites recognized that the claiming of a people's inheritance relied on a recognition and reclaiming of their cultural heritage. Reparations could take the form of previous compensatory strategies for African Americans and focus principally on material goods— the forty acres and a mule proposed for former slaves at the time of emancipation. Such material payback has been a dominant aspect of the reparations paid to other populations that have been harmed by their governments. In the Luxembourg Agreement of 1952, for example, Germany paid out the equivalent of one billion dollars in reparations for crimes committed by the Third Reich against the Jewish people for their material losses and suffering. Even in the United States there has been some partial payment on the debt. In 1994 Governor Lawton Chiles of Florida signed a bill granting $2.1 million in reparations to the descendants of the black victims of Rosewood. The Rosewood massacre of 1923 involved white lynch mobs that murdered six blacks during a week of violence and hate. Those who survived the massacre were driven into the swamps.

But reparations should be directed to more than material compensation. The long-term effects of three hundred years of slavery, abuse, discrimination, and historical distortion call for more than just a cash payment to individuals. The recovery of cultural identity should lead to the end that every African American has a prideful knowledge of and ownership of African American history. Moreover, ownership of African American history should identify the prominent role African Americans have played in shaping American history and culture. Although entitlement to a debt owed is one way of conceiving of reparations, from a Joshua perspective reparations should be viewed as claiming ownership of that which has already been fought for. Alongside material repayment would be the internalization of an attitude of possessing that which one already has but has been lost, stolen, or hidden.

It also is important to recognize that the acquisition of reparations is not an end in itself, just as in Joshua the acquisition of the land was not an end in itself. The acquisition of the land was delivery on a previous promise, but was also the beginning of a renewed covenant between God and the ancient Israelites. Certain future expectations went along with the fulfillment of the promise, expectations that had primarily to do with the faithfulness the ancient Israelites were to exercise in their appropriation of the land. The recovery of a cultural identity and an increased sense of connectedness were to lead to the development of a nation whose example would be a light to other nations. The recovery of a sense of pride demands that the contributions African Americans made to the building of America be fully recognized. The current status of African Americans should be reinterpreted in light of the intergenerational effects of slavery. And the newer forms of racism must be challenged as the battle for survival and liberation continues.[8] The black church can play an important role in this recovery and reinterpretation process. As the black church takes on its historical functions as a vehicle for protest, a teller of the story, and a community of life together, it can add a unique spiritual dimension to the reparations enterprise.

---

[8]Two examples of the newer forms of racism are found in coded language and exceptionalist examples. In Chicago recently a Catholic school athletic league voted to not include in the league a school in the heart of the black community. The reason given was that of "safety." Cognizant of the fact that it is not politically correct to reject on the basis of color, the athletic league rejected on the basis of safety for parents, children, coaches, and umpires. To its credit the Archdiocese of Chicago renounced the action by the athletic league and deemed it racist activity. At a speech at the University of Pennsylvania Derrick Bell pointed out that the extraordinary accomplishments of some blacks are used as examples by some whites to argue that no special assistance is needed by blacks to achieve success. If an A. Leon Higginbotham or Colin Powell or Condoleezza Rice can make it, other blacks can do it too. See also Thomas F. Pettigrew, "New Patterns of Racism: The Different Worlds of 1984 and 1964," *Rutgers Law Review* 37 (1985): 674, in which he argues that the modern forms of racism have become more subtle, indirect, procedural, and ostensibly nonracial.

The Black Church and a Vision for the Future

One of the real challenges associated with recovering a cultural identity through reparations is the dominant theme that slavery plays in the reparations enterprise. Because slavery looms large as the cause of the disparity between African Americans and whites, reparations are intended to reduce the negative impact of slavery on African Americans' ability to break free of slavery's debilitating legacy. It would be very easy for slavery and its aftermath to completely engulf African American cultural identity. When the future of African Americans is defined by the campaign to be adequately compensated for the labor they exerted in slavery, there is the possibility to think that the future vision is limited to their cultural identity as former slaves. Such a vision describes who blacks were but does not adequately define who blacks are or who blacks hope to be. The creation of transformative visions that take persons from their debilitating past and transport them to a vital future are fundamental to African American religion.

Through story and ritual the black church, along with other religious movements, has empowered African Americans to transcend the limiting structures of the material world. In these more transcendent realities African Americans have been able to see themselves not as slaves but as participants in a world constituted by justice, peace, and plenty. In these visions are streets of gold, reunions with loved ones, new clothes, and peace of mind. It is a vision of the way things "ought to be." Now "ought to be" includes a denunciation (signification) of what is or has been, but it is more. "Ought to be" is a description of an ideal whose construction moves beyond the void of mere deconstruction. The constructive dimension of "ought to be" is the locus of its capacity to excite and inspire. Moreover, the moral authority of "ought to be" carries with it a moral power whose force has the capacity to break out of imposed negative identities. In this new place with the power to create a more life-giving existence, African Americans can fashion an identity that transcends the limits imposed by the dominant society. The black church continues to have a role as a transformer and transcender of limiting identities. The black church must bring the weight of its new life agenda to the reparations campaign.

A vision for the future points to the process of becoming. Rather than focusing exclusively on making up for the past, the future vision should describe that for which one is striving. The question then becomes: what do African Americans hope to achieve as a result of reparations? What goal are reparations intended to help achieve? The goal should not be limited to full restitution. Rather, there should be a vision of what African Americans will become as a result of payment of the debt. The black church has historically helped African Americans vision a future for themselves. The overarching principle driving the vision has been freedom and equality of all persons under God, and that historical vision has served to motivate

African Americans for three hundred years. However, such a vision is too general and unspecific for a people about to claim their inheritance, a people whose cultural identity and sense of connectedness to one another are at risk.

In the face of sociopolitical forces that put at risk the survival of African Americans, what can the black church add to the reparations movement that stems the tide of black genocide? In the face of a rising pluralism within the African American community that has coalesced into a cultural politics of difference, how can the black church steer reparations in a way that preserves a rich legacy and history? As African Americans experience increasing alienation from one another, are there perspectives and rituals that the black church can employ that restore a sense of connectedness? In the face of increasing nihilism and despair, can the black church help fashion a vision for the future that provides hope? The answer to these questions is yes, but first the black church must engage in a campaign to reinforce its role as a pragmatic, practical, and political agent in the life of African Americans.

The Black Church—A History of Pragmatic Agency

Since its inception the black church has melded its theological and religious roles with that of its roles as a pragmatic strategist, practical activist, and political power broker. The church in the bush was not only an occasion for praise, it was a place for devising how to fight the institution of slavery. Sometimes that meant planning individual and group escapes. At other times it meant sharing information about white folks' ways so as to avoid trouble. And at still other times it was a way of handing on to the next generation the rituals, language, and cultural identity brought from Africa. Even the founding of the historically black churches was as much rebellion against white oppression as it was desire to praise the Lord in one's own unique way. The black church today, whether part of predominantly white denominations or independent black denominations, continues the battle to praise God through social uplift and political action. In the past, slavery, Jim Crow, and segregation made clear who the enemy was and what needed to be done. Now the fragmentation within the African American community and the nuanced ways in which racism is making itself known[9] call for a more rigorously conceived and thoroughly examined approach to the achievement of freedom and equality of all persons under God.

---

[9]See Pettigrew, "New Patterns of Racism," 686. Pettigrew says the new racism rejects gross stereotypes and blatant discrimination but is still made manifest in the following ways: (1) normative compliance without internalization of new behavioral norms of racial acceptance, (2) indirect "micro-aggressions" against blacks, which are expressed in avoidance of face-to-face interaction with blacks and in opposition to racial change for ostensible nonracial reasons, (3) a sense of subjective threat from racial change, and (4) individualistic conceptions of how opportunity and social stratification operate in American society.

Inherent in the campaign for reparations is the location of African Americans in a dependent position. Granted, the call for reparations can be viewed as the powerful demand of a people for what they have earned and is rightfully owed to them. It is a sign of their dignity and worth. However, the fact still remains that blacks are seeking redress from whites, are dependent on them for redress. The implication is that freedom and equality will result from the granting of reparations by white America. How dependent do blacks want to be or have to be in order to secure a sense of freedom and equality? The history and legacy of the black church show it to be an independent institution of African Americans' own making that has made a significant contribution to the survival and thriving of a people. I believe much of the loyalty and devotion that African Americans have to the black church is precisely due to its standing as an independent agent in the life of blacks in America. Moreover, that same independent institution has played a crucial role in combating the assaults of racism on African Americans. The black church has helped produce exceptional artists, educators, businesses, banks, centers of higher education, and a people of character in spite of a dominant society that espouses the idea that anything black is begrimed and dirty.

The black church brings a serious question to the reparations campaign: How much reliance do we want to have on reparations for the achievement of our goals, when the example of the black church demonstrates that there can be exceptional achievement within the black community when it relies on its own resources and sense of self? The proponents of reparations argue that without reparations African Americans will never be able to make up the gap that exists between black America and the rest of America. However, if the catch-up depends exclusively on white largesse, the closing of the gap could include the unwanted outcome of a diminished sense of self-sufficiency and agency over one's life. With that as a potential outcome, how much do African Americans want to buy into reparations? Again let me state that I am in support of reparations, but the reparations campaign must include a rigorous and critical look at the benefits/cost dimensions of any reparations program.

A Critical Joshua Perspective

As both a conjure and a signifier the book of Joshua acts as an instrument for critical evaluation of African American culture and life. As we have seen, a Joshua perspective can be applied to concepts regarding black cultural identity formation and gender relationships in the African American community in order to critically examine the ways in which survival and liberation can best be pursued in those areas. From these earlier discussions we can begin to construct a framework for a critical Joshua perspective that can be applied not only to the issue of reparations but to a variety of concerns that impact on African American life and culture. Faith-based social services, public education alternatives, and congressional redistricting are but a few of the topics about which there is fierce debate, and clarity is needed as to how the black community should proceed in these areas of concern. A critical Joshua perspective offers a framework and guidelines for how to examine these issues and points to ways of articulating future movement on them.

A critical Joshua perspective would include the following features:

• A survival *and* liberation thrust
• Collective cultural identity formation that honors difference
• Self-determination
• Faithful adherence to God's promise of full humanity

Any vision for the future for African Americans must take seriously the threat to survival that exists on an ongoing basis for black Americans. At any given moment in history the forward thrust of freedom and liberation can be reversed. Gains on any number of different socioeconomic fronts can easily become losses. The progress of a hundred years can easily be wiped out with a presidential executive order, a failure to pass on the African American tradition, global realignments, and demographic shifts that reorder priorities. Survival for African Americans is not guaranteed *unless* there is a continuous campaign to struggle for a people's existence.

But mere survival is not the life that God promises to African Americans. The promise is for full humanity. Consequently, beyond mere existence African Americans must continue to fight for a place and a space where their dignity and destiny can flourish. In that location, which is principally an internal consciousness, African Americans generate the power and confidence to ward off the larger society's efforts at passive and active genocide through a variety of forms of "lynching." In that location, African Americans live fully the life that has been promised to them by God, a life with cultural pride and the power of self-determination.

A critical Joshua perspective values both a collective cultural identity and the different ways in which persons contribute to that collective cultural identity. One without the other is unacceptable. A collective cultural identity that does not allow for difference is coercively abusive and denies itself the fullness and richness of all its resources. A cultural politics of difference that celebrates difference without a concomitant commitment to contribute to and participate in the creation of a collective cultural identity chooses a limited goal of individual expression. Moreover, when the cultural politics of difference shifts into individualism, the survival of the individual and the group are at risk. The survival and liberation of a people are primary, and a collective cultural identity helps to ensure the vitality of group life. At times collective cultural identity formation can exert too much pressure by stifling individual expression. Although there will always be tension between the two, a critical Joshua perspective seeks to hold the two in tension without renunciation on either side.

Living Free, Making Choices, and Acting with a Sense of Agency

From a critical Joshua perspective self-determination means having the power to live free, make choices, and act with a sense of one's own agency. These three elements of self-determination are very much intertwined with one another. For the purpose of this discussion, I have broken them out heuristically to highlight certain points. Living free is more than not living enslaved. Living free means having a full range of opportunities and possibilities available. It means crossing over Jordan into the promised land and all that it holds in front of you. Self-determination, at its base, assumes that whatever one wants to be or do, one has the freedom to be or do.

Self-determination includes having the freedom to make choices. When options are available, there is both the opportunity and the need for choices to be made. Without self-determination others make choices for us; with self-determination we make choices for ourselves. There is an obligational dimension to self-determination associated with choice making. Having the opportunity to make choices but failing to do so is squandering a gift given to us from God. The Joshua story is full of situations where the ancient Israelites had choices to make in the course of their conquest campaign. The book ends with a choice that Joshua puts to the people about whom they will serve in the future. Just having the opportunity to make a choice is a sign of freedom. But a critical Joshua perspective calls on all who would live free to make correct choices—that is, choices that are in keeping with God's destiny for African Americans: full humanity and cultural fulfillment.

Finally, self-determination includes a sense of agency. In chapter 2, I introduced Archie Smith's definition of a sense of agency: "a belief in the ability to make decisions and act on them, to resist, create anew, or otherwise exercise power to influence how things will turn out."[10] In addition to the freedom of opportunities, the availability of options, and the possibility to make choices, self-determination includes the belief that one can act on the opportunities and choices that one has. Self-determination means possessing confidence in one's capacity to fulfill the opportunities and choices that one has. Camped in the plains of Moab, the ancient Israelites both had the opportunity and had made the choice to enter into Canaan. Yet they remained fixed in that place until their sense of agency was aroused by God: "Now proceed to cross the Jordan, you and all this people, into the land that I am giving to them, to the Israelites" (Josh. 1:2). Reminded

---

[10]Archie Smith, *Navigating the Deep River: Spirituality in African American Families* (Cleveland: United Church Press, 1997), 27.

of the promise of God and encouraged to be of good courage, the ancient Israelites appropriated a sense of agency about the campaign that empowered them for the upcoming battles. With this sense of agency the ancient Israelites created a new place for themselves to live free and live out their destiny.

A Vision for the Future

Using reparations as a framework and resource and equipped with a critical Joshua perspective, we now ask, What should a vision for the future for African Americans look like at the turn of the twenty-first century? I would like to answer this question using the black church as a structural framework for the construction of my response.

It seems to me that a vision for the future of black America includes the following four elements: (1) equipping for survival and liberation, (2) adopting all our children, (3) gathering to remember and give thanks, and (4) continually revisioning the future. These four elements are not present as a complete representation of all of what the visions for the future should include. They are, however, four elements that emerge from the discussion presented in this book.

Equipping for Survival and Liberation. What are the resources that will be needed by African Americans to live into a future that guarantees survival and liberation? A chief resource will be improved health for African Americans. If the black community can decrease black infant mortality, reduce the incidence of life-threatening disease, and foster better health habits, then black survival is almost automatically guaranteed. In the past the black church has played a major role in the healthy well-being of its communities and continues to do so today. In the future the health ministries of the black church must have a dual focus of targeting particularly life-threatening health concerns and preventing illness through health education programs.

In the Introduction I presented data that demonstrate that the health of African Americans is worsening in certain categories. Consider, however, the case of prostate cancer in Detroit, where the survival gap between black men and white men has narrowed. Between 1990 and 1995 cancer was diagnosed before it spread outside the prostate in 38 percent of African Americans and 48 percent of whites. From 1996 to 1999, however, the rate of prostate-confined cancer was 54 percent in blacks and 62 percent in whites. So there was not only a narrowing of the gap between blacks and whites but also an overall increase in the survival rate for African American men, which reached above 50 percent. Dr. Fernando J. Bianco, Jr., of Wayne State University in Detroit reported these findings at a meeting of the American Urological Association in May 2001. Dr. Bianco attributes the success of the prostate cancer reduction in African American males to a prostate cancer awareness campaign carried out in black churches in Detroit during the 1990s. Obviously the work of the black churches in Detroit had an effect. And if the black church through its health ministries can address prostate cancer, in all probability it can help reduce the incidence of other diseases and disorders.

The primary enemies of African American health are violence, infant mortality, heart disease, diabetes, high blood pressure, and HIV/AIDS. All black churches should have a health ministry division that addresses these health concerns. The attack on these threats to African American survival needs to be three-pronged: (1) education, (2) screening, and (3) spiritual healing. Prevention is the most effective tool in fighting disease and illness, and prevention education focused on the chief enemies of African American health will have the greatest impact on reducing those maladies. Periodic campaigns to take blood pressures on Sunday mornings and to encourage screening exams for breast cancer (mammograms), heart problems (electrocardiograms), and prostate cancer (PSA test) should be pursued from the pulpit, as well as in religious education and special programs. Prenatal counseling, conflict resolution classes, and safe sex discussions should be a part of healthy lifestyle conversations taking place in a variety of formal and informal settings in the church. Teaming up with a medical center can greatly aid in the coordination and cost reduction of these health education and screening initiatives. Long before Larry Dossey and others scientifically affirmed the power of prayer to heal, black churches prayed and laid hands on people for healing. Healing services that are either a part of the Sunday morning worship or separate times of worship constitute an essential ingredient to a church's health ministry. There is much that human beings can do to help facilitate health and healing, but the ultimate outcome of those efforts rests in the hands of spiritual forces that have the power to cure and make whole.

Doing battle with powers and principalities that do not have the best interests of African Americans at heart requires that a Joshua people identify and make the most use of their collective connection to one another. Much has been written about the extended family in the African American community. The references to extended family apply not only to blood ties but also to what has been termed as *fictive kinship,* which is a "kinship-like connection between and among persons in a society, not related by blood or marriage, who have maintained essential reciprocal social or economic relationships."[11] The fictive kinship system has been a principal way in which African Americans have been able to preserve a life-enhancing cultural identity. In the fictive kinship system persons acquire the values, worldview, and rituals that sustain life in that culture. The fictive kinship system has also played the role of a mediating structure that helped African Americans navigate between the dominant culture and their own individual

[11]S. Fordham, "Racelessness as a Factor in Black Students' School Success: Pragmatic Strategy or Pyrrhic Victory?" *Harvard Educational Review* 58, no. 1 (1988):56.

families of origin. When a person is separated from family, the fictive kinship system gives encouragement, support, and healing in the face of the hurt, injury, or confusion encountered in the dominant culture. In addition, the fictive kinship system is a means of protest and opposition to the images, interpretations, and valuations made by the larger society.

In the face of socioeconomic reversals, confusing developments in black cultural identity, and disconnection among African Americans, greater emphasis must be placed in the future on recognizing and utilizing the fictive kinship system. Within this fictive kinship system African Americans should focus on the primary task of adopting all our children.

Adopting All Our Children

Too many of our children are dying too young. They are dying physically (infant mortality, HIV/AIDS, adolescent suicide, homicide, and abuse) and they are dying in their spirits (depression, hopelessness, dropping out of high school, and drug use). The phrase "it takes a village to raise a child" has become somewhat of a cliché, but the underlying truth of the statement remains: more than a nuclear family is needed to bring a child into adulthood. In the African American community the loss of our children reflects a need to provide more care and protection. This additional care and protection will have to come from all of us. Whether that child is growing up in a poverty-stricken single-parent household or a wealthy household with an intact marital unit, the fact of the matter is that all black children are vulnerable to the death-dealing circumstances of being black in America today. All African American adults have a responsibility to adopt the children around them. By adoption I do not mean formal, legal adoption. What I mean is an informal adoption in which the adult takes responsibility for looking out for and looking after the interests of that child. Some adults, because of abundant material resources and availability of time, will be able to provide much, others less, but all have something to give. A word of encouragement, a minute of time, or a little advice all can go a long way in fostering hope in a child. Nathan McCall writes eloquently about the kind of fictive kinship attention to which I am alluding:

> We kids hated that surrogate system. It seemed that everybody was so nosy and bent on making sure we didn't get away with anything. It was only years later, when black communities as we knew them started falling apart, that I came to understand the system for the hidden blessings it contained: It had built-in mechanisms for reinforcing values and trying to prevent us from becoming the hellions some of us turned out to be.[12]

---

[12]Nathan McCall, *Makes Me Wanna Holler: A Young Black Man in America* (New York: Random House, 1994), 9.

Certainly through the youth ministries of the black church, encouragement, guidance, and protection can easily be provided. However, the black youth who are at greater risk are outside the walls of the church, so that is where the black church needs to make a commitment for the future. A Joshua church needs to become a Joshua family in which all the children have kinship with all the adults in and outside the church. More formal programs of mentoring or rites of passage may be the way in which some churches choose to live out this commitment to raising children. In addition, though, I would suggest that black churches encourage their members to look to the children who are close by their homes and apartments and "adopt" those children as the ones in whom they will take a special interest. In that way a Joshua people help ensure that no child wanders off and becomes lost.

Gathering to Remember

Every Sunday morning millions of black Christians gather to worship God. In their worship they sing songs of praise, confess their sins, receive the word of God, give thanks, and renew their commitment to Christ. In the process the parishioners receive new life in Christ and begin to live transformed lives. The ritual is repeated every week, recognizing that the Christian life is in need of renewal on an ongoing basis. The salvation that was won for Christians in the one-time act of Jesus' death is sustained in the Christian's life by remembering how that salvation is made manifest in life day by day, from week to week. In the process of linking their faith tradition with the historical events of their lives African Americans have contributed to the cultural history of a people. The songs, chants, prayers, stories, ritualized movements, ways of making meaning, and institutions that have emerged from the melding of religious tradition and lived experience have contributed to the rich and diverse product we have come to know as African American culture. The ritual of gathering to remember, to give praise and thanks, and to renew one's life is not limited to black Christians, of course. Blacks of other faith traditions also engage in regularly scheduled rituals of renewal and recommitment. Whether the faith tradition is Christian, Muslim, Voodoo, Rastafarian, or Humanist, there exists a faith tradition linked with lived experience that has also contributed to the creation of African American culture.

Over the years the collective cultural production of black Americans has accumulated, comprising religious and nonreligious elements (although a strong argument could be made that the original African worldview that did not bifurcate the sacred and the secular permeates African American culture and makes the line of demarcation between religious and nonreligious in African American culture quite faint at times). But while the collective cultural production of black America has been accumulating over the years, there has been a drain on the collective cultural memory of

African Americans as well. Cultural creations that are linked with particular historical events often lose their interpretive and transforming power the farther away they move in time from the historical event itself. In addition, African American cultural memory has had to contend with competing cultural memories of the dominant group and that group's propensity to denigrate, deny, and dismiss the cultural productions of African Americans. The total effect is that much of our collective cultural memory is either lost, hidden, or misappropriated. In order to recapture the vital and life-giving features of our collective culture, African Americans must engage in what Toni Morrison calls a "process of cultural archaeology."[13] The archaeological enterprise seeks to recover the cultural productions and artifacts that have become lost to a collective cultural memory. Gathering to remember God's mighty acts of deliverance in both the distant and recent past restores and reinvigorates the collective cultural memory. For in remembering that involves a full memory recall of the drama of the historical moment, the powerful presence of a deliverer, and the excitement of a transformed reality, all come together to give hope for the present moment. If God has done it once, God can do it again. If God can deliver Daniel, God can deliver me. If God can make a home for the ancient Israelites across the Jordan, God can create a home for African Americans in America today. In religious education, preaching, and worship the black church should engage in the archeological task of recovering collective cultural memory so that a people can have access to the vital cultural heritage that has been at the heart of their survival and liberation.

In addition to archaeological cultural recovery, the remembering task for the black church in the future is that of bringing African Americans closer together as a people. In this sense the remembering task is one of "re-membering," putting back together parts of the body that have been separated from one another. If there is to be survival and liberation for African Americans in America in the future, the disconnectedness of African Americans must be overcome. This is another way in which the Joshua conquest for today has less to do with fighting an external enemy and more to do with an internal consciousness struggle within the black community. African Americans have to find ways to be more loving, supportive, and caring of one another. Commitments to one another must be lived out responsibly and with integrity. African Americans are accountable to one another to create a sense of peoplehood where collective black culture has the power to create strong cultural identities in its members, especially the children. The re-membering task includes balancing the interests of the individual and the interests of the group so that each can mutually energize the other.

---

[13]Toni Morrison, "The Site of Memory," in *Out There: Marginalization and Contemporary Cultures,* ed. Russell Ferguson, Martha Gever, Trinh T. Minh-ha, and Cornel West (Cambridge, Mass.: MIT Press, 1994), 302.

What would it look like if the black church took seriously its responsibility to foster the two kinds of remembering just indicated? Perhaps part of the worship service would include a time when persons would in small groups or as a family tell the story of how God had been active in the past week to promote their survival and liberation. This fifteen-minute period of sharing might be preceded by a storyteller's recitation of a moment in black history when a spiritual force was present in the deliverance of African Americans. The personal recitation of memory, along with the group historical recitation of memory, would be linked with the larger tradition's biblical recitation of memory in the form of scripture and sermon, which would then make for a comprehensive, multidimensional recovery of collective cultural memory.

Such a change in worship format might even suggest a change in church architecture. A Joshua church might not be exclusively focused on the pulpit– that is, a row of fixed pews all facing forward with a pulpit at center stage. Instead, a Joshua church might have movable seating where the gathered body could meet as a whole and as small groups, and even when gathered as a whole could give themselves the sense of being a whole body by sitting facing one another instead of looking at the impersonal backs of one another's heads.

Leadership in a Joshua church would be shared. As was the case in the first chapter of the book of Joshua, the opportunity to deliver the message from God was not exclusively given to Joshua. The message was given to Joshua, who then handed it down to other leaders, who were given the responsibility to deliver God's message to the remainder of the people. Might not black pastors share more of their power and responsibility, not only to spare them from overextension but also to enhance the capacity of a people to live responsibly and accountably with one another?

Continually Revisioning the Future

If there is to be a future for African Americans in America, that future must always be reexamined in light of current realities and projected trends. No vision of the future can last forever. It can never anticipate all the events, twists, and turns that life inevitably brings. Consequently, any vision of the future has a limited shelf life and must be revised in order to have power and relevance. So the first element in any vision for the future for African Americans must include a commitment to reexamining the vision on an ongoing basis. Otherwise, African Americans risk confinement to a vision whose potential for promoting survival and liberation is nonexistent. If a vision for the future no longer holds the potential to provide life and home, the appropriation of that vision needs to be called into question. The reexamination of a less-than-vital vision does not necessarily mean that the vision as a whole has to be scrapped. Rather, some parts or dimensions of it may need to be altered somewhat. In any case, the vision that was proposed in the past requires constant evaluation to determine whether or not its efficacy still exists for the present moment. If it does, commitment to that vision remains. If it does not, a change needs to be made.

Dreaming and visioning are the stock-in-trade of the black church. Since its beginning as an "invisible institution," the black church has lifted up visions of a better time and place for African Americans than the oppressive experience of America. These visions have sustained a people through the brutality of slavery, the ignominy of Jim Crow discrimination, and the pervasive presence of racism that continues to linger. The black church still has a visioning function to play, but it must do so with two changes given the present situation.

First, the black church must recognize the real threat to African American survival and fashion a vision that focuses more on the here and now. It is a shift in emphasis, because the vision needed for today is more short term than long term. It is a vision that fashions a home for its Joshua people here and now where they are. The other re-visioning that needs to take place is related to the permanence of racism.[14] There will continually be new and different forms of racism and race prejudice in America. Any vision for the future for African Americans must take this factor into account and include strategies for combating the more recent manifestations of racism's menace.

There are two areas in which past visions of the future for African Americans should be changed for the present moment. Each is related to politics, but each reflects different aspects of the political sphere. The civil rights movement envisioned that a more fair and just America would emerge with access to the right to vote and the use of the courts as the vehicle for redress of wrongs. Black churches actively participated in voter registration drives and financially supported the NAACP and other organizations committed to bringing civil rights cases before the courts. As part of a larger vision for the survival and liberation of blacks in America, these strategies made sense and, even more importantly, produced the desired results: the freedom to vote and increased civil rights.

The 2000 national election and the reparations movement indicate that strategies within the larger vision of the future must be altered. The role of racism in black voting is more subtle and procedurally based than it has been in the past. Rather than deny blacks the vote through Jim Crow legislation in order to disenfranchise them, the newer forms of racism deny blacks the vote through outdated voting machines that break down, inadequately designed and maintained punch card voting devices, and the refusal to provide more accurate and mistake-proof electronic voting machines in black communities. Black churches need to now envision

---

[14]See Derrick Bell, *Faces at the Bottom of the Well: The Permanence of Racism* (New York: Basic Books, 1992).

themselves fighting for the right to vote in new ways, which include the demand for voting machines that will actually count the votes cast by blacks.

The pro-black sympathies and the sensibilities of the Warren court of the sixties no longer exist. Twenty years of conservative federal judicial appointments during the Nixon, Reagan, and Bush administrations have created a federal court system that is antagonistic to the claims of blacks for redress and equal protection under the law. Consequently, as the black church becomes more involved in the reparations movement, the focus for redress needs to shift from the federal courts to local legislative bodies. The courts in their recent decisions[15] have made clear that either they do not believe in reparations or they believe that they do not have the power to adjudicate the matter. As a part of its revisioning strategy the black church needs to not turn to the courts but join with other organizations in their petitions to legislative bodies such as state and federal legislatures, where there has been more willingness to entertain reparations claims. These are but two examples of ways in which the visioning for the future for African Americans must continually be reevaluated in order to secure a more viable future.

---

[15]See Robert Westley, "Many Billions Gone: Is It Time to Reconsider the Case for Black Reparations?" *Boston College Law Review* 40, no. 1 (1998): 429–76.

※ A BRIEF POSTSCRIPT

As indicated earlier, a primary element in the vision for the future for African Americans is the need for a collective commitment by a people to strive together for their survival and liberation. This may appear to be isolationist. What about relationships with other racial/ethnic groups? For now the present emphasis in America on multiculturalism and diversity needs to take a backseat to the more pressing concerns of survival and liberation in the black community. If African Americans participate in those crosscultural enterprises without first guaranteeing a location for themselves, it will lead to a greater sense of dislocation and disempowerment.

America is becoming more diverse and culturally interactive. African Americans cannot avoid and should not resist the increased crossing of cultural boundaries that are occurring in schools, at work, and even in houses of worship. Moreover, it is inevitable that such crossculturality will mutually impact and transform cultures. However, African Americans must have a substantive culture in place in order to engage in the multicultural enterprise with integrity. Too often black culture has had to disappear in order to come into contact with other cultures. And if diversity is going to work properly, the cultural identity of the various cultures must have a strength of presence so that each can participate with equal status and effect. Consequently, there is a new kind of double consciousness that African Americans must have today. The previous double consciousness DuBois coined in the twentieth century described African Americans with two conflicting identities—one American, the other Negro—that existed in one body. The new double consciousness of the twenty-first century for African Americans is that of two cultural identities, one in diversity with other cultures and one diverse in its common cultural expression. The two cultural identities are not so much in conflict with each other, but they require critical discernment as persons move between the two. It will require a strong spiritual force to empower persons to navigate between the two cultural realities without getting lost or shipwrecked.

For African Americans today the message in Joshua is to keep before them the faith, culture, and traditions that have enabled them to survive and overcome all that America has promulgated to deny African Americans full humanity. The question that African Americans must wrestle with is: Will the current campaigns to foster a more diverse and multicultural reality in America empower blacks to more successfully stem the tide of black genocide and contribute to a greater sense of homecoming? This is where the critical Joshua perspective comes into play. Will America's thrust to acknowledge its diversity further the African American survival *and* liberation thrust? Is there room for black collective cultural identity formation that honors difference? Does the celebration of diversity and multiculturalism promote self-determination within the black community? And do efforts at crossculturalism reflect faithful adherence to God's promise of full humanity for African Americans? I believe America's movement toward recognizing and celebrating its diversity could further African American survival and liberation, as well as support the promise of full humanity for individual blacks. However, I am not as sure that multiculturalism will promote black collective cultural formation or black self-determination for blacks as a people.

❋ INDEX